Unit
Assessments

Table of Contents

Unit Assessments

The *Unit Assessments* component is an integral part of the complete assessment program aligned with *Wonders* and state standards.

Purpose

This component reports on the outcome of student learning. As students complete each unit of the reading program, they will be assessed on their understanding of key instructional content and their ability to write to source texts/stimuli. The results serve as a summative assessment by providing a status of current achievement in relation to student progress through the curriculum. The results of the assessments can be used to inform subsequent instruction, aid in making leveling and grouping decisions, and point toward areas in need of reteaching or remediation.

Focus

Unit Assessments focuses on key areas of English Language Arts—comprehension of literature and informational text, vocabulary acquisition and use, command of the conventions of the English language, and genre writing in response to sources.

Each unit assessment also provides students familiarity with the item types, the test approaches, and the increased rigor associated with the advances in state-mandated high-stakes assessments.

Test Administration

Each unit assessment should be administered once the instruction for the specific unit is completed. Make copies of the unit assessment for the class. You will need copies of the answer key pages that feature the scoring charts for each student taking the assessment, which provide a place to list student scores. The data from each unit assessment charts student progress and underscores strengths and weaknesses.

This component is the pencil-and-paper version of the assessment. You can administer the online version of the test, which allows for technology-enhanced item functionality.

NOTE: Due to time constraints, you may wish to administer the unit assessment over multiple days. For example, students can complete the 20-item test on the first day and complete the performance task on another. For planning purposes, the recommended time for each performance task is 90–100 minutes over two back-to-back sessions. During the first session, provide students 30–40 minutes to read the stimulus materials and answer the research questions. During the second session, provide students 60–70 minutes for planning, writing, and editing their responses. If desired, provide students a short break between sessions. If you decide to break up administration by assessment sections, please remember to withhold those sections of the test students are not completing to ensure test validity.

After each student has a copy of the assessment, provide a version of the following directions:

Teacher Introduction

Say: *Write your name on the question pages for this assessment.* (When students are finished, continue with the directions.) *You will read three texts and answer questions about them. In the next part of the test, you will read a student draft that you will revise or edit for the correct grammar, mechanics, and usage. In the final part of the test, you will read sources, answer questions about them, and write a response based on the assignment you will find, which will ask you to use those sources in your writing.*

Read each part of the test carefully. For multiple-choice questions, circle the letter next to the correct answer or answers. For other types of questions, look carefully at the directions. You may be asked to match items, circle or underline choices, or complete a chart. For the constructed-response question, write your response on the lines provided. For the performance task, write your response to the assignment on separate sheets of paper. When you have completed the assessment, put your pencil down and turn the pages over. You may begin now.

Answer procedural questions during the assessment, but do not provide any assistance on the items or selections. Have extra paper on hand for students to use for their performance task responses. After the class has completed the assessment, ask students to verify that their names are written on the necessary pages.

Assessment Items

Unit assessments feature the following item types—selected response (SR), multiple selected response (MSR), evidence-based selected response (EBSR), constructed response (CR), and technology-enhanced items (TE). (Please note that the print versions of TE items are available in this component; the full functionality of the items is available only through the online assessment.) This variety of item types provides multiple methods of assessing student understanding, allows for deeper investigation into skills and strategies, and provides students an opportunity to become familiar with the kinds of questions they will encounter in state-mandated summative assessments.

Performance Tasks

Each unit features a performance task (PT) assessment in a previously taught genre. Students will complete two examples of each task type by the end of the year.

- Narrative
  - Students craft a narrative using information from the sources.

- Informational
  - Students generate a thesis based on the sources and use information from the sources to explain this thesis.

- Opinion
  - Students analyze the ideas in sources and make a claim that they support using the sources.

Each PT assesses standards that address comprehension, research skills, genre writing, and the use of standard English language conventions (ELC). The stimulus texts and research questions in each task build toward the goal of the final writing topic.

Overview

- Students will read three texts in each assessment and respond to items focusing on comprehension skills, literary elements, text features, and vocabulary strategies. These items assess the ability to access meaning from the text and demonstrate understanding of unknown and multiple-meaning words and phrases.

- Students will then read a student draft that requires corrections or clarifications to its use of the conventions of standard English language.

- Students are then presented with a performance task assessment.

Each test item in *Unit Assessments* (as well as in progress monitoring and benchmark assessments) has a Depth of Knowledge (DOK) level assigned to it.

Vocabulary items

DOK 1: Use word parts (affixes, roots) to determine the meaning of an unknown word.

DOK 2: Use context or print/digital resources to determine the meaning of an unknown or multiple-meaning word; use context to understand figurative language.

Comprehension items

DOK 1: Identify/locate information in the text.

DOK 2: Analyze text structures/literary elements.

DOK 3: Make inferences using text evidence and analyze author's craft.

DOK 4: Respond using multiple texts.

Revising and Editing items

DOK 1: Edit to fix errors

DOK 2: Revise for clarity and coherence.

Each unit assessment features three "cold reads" on which the comprehension and vocabulary assessment items are based. These selections reflect the unit theme and genre-studies to support the focus of the classroom instruction. Texts fall within the Lexile band 830L-1010L. Complexity on this quantitative measure grows throughout the units, unless a qualitative measure supports text placement outside a lockstep Lexile continuum.

Comprehension

Comprehension items assess student understanding of the text through the use of the comprehension skills, literary elements, and text features taught throughout the unit.

Teacher Introduction

Vocabulary

Vocabulary items ask students to demonstrate their ability to uncover the meanings of unknown and multiple-meaning words and phrases using vocabulary strategies.

English Language Conventions

Five items in each unit ask students to demonstrate their command of the conventions of standard English.

Performance Task

Students complete one performance task per unit, which includes research questions and a final written response in the specified task genre.

Scoring

Each unit assessment totals 35 points. Comprehension and vocabulary items are worth two points each. Constructed-response and multi-part items should be answered correctly in full, though you may choose to provide partial credit. Revising and editing items are worth one point each. Use the scoring chart at the bottom of the answer key to record each student's score. Note that the performance task is scored separately, as described below.

For the constructed-response items, assign a score using the correct response parameters provided in the answer key along with the scoring rubrics shown below. Responses that show a complete lack of understanding or are left blank should be given a *0*.

Short Response Score 2: The response is well-crafted and concise and shows a thorough understanding of the underlying skill. Appropriate text evidence is used to answer the question.

Short Response Score 1: The response shows partial understanding of the underlying skill. Text evidence is featured, though examples are too general.

Each unit performance task is a separate 15-point assessment. The three research items are worth a total of five points, broken down as indicated in the scoring charts. Score the written response holistically on a 10-point scale, using the rubrics on the following pages:

- 4 points for purpose/organization [P/O]

- 4 points for evidence/elaboration [E/E] or development/elaboration [D/E]

- 2 points for English language conventions [C]

- Unscorable or 0-point responses are unrelated to the topic, illegible, contain little or no writing, or show little to no command of the conventions of standard English.

Use the top-score anchor paper response provided in the answer key for each test for additional scoring guidance.

NARRATIVE PERFORMANCE TASK SCORING RUBRIC

Score	Purpose/Organization	Development/Elaboration	Conventions
4	• **fully sustained** organization; **clear** focus • effective, unified plot • effective development of setting, characters, point of view • transitions clarify relationships between and among ideas • logical sequence of events • effective opening and closing	• **effective** elaboration with details, dialogue, description • clear expression of experiences and events • effective use of relevant source material • effective use of various narrative techniques • effective use of sensory, concrete, and figurative language	
3	• **adequately sustained** organization; **generally maintained** focus • evident plot with loose connections • adequate development of setting, characters, point of view • adequate use of transitional strategies • adequate sequence of events • adequate opening and closing	• **adequate** elaboration with details, dialogue, description • adequate expression of experiences and events • adequate use of source material • adequate use of various narrative techniques • adequate use of sensory, concrete, and figurative language	
2	• **somewhat sustained** organization; **uneven** focus • inconsistent plot with evident flaws • uneven development of setting, characters, point of view • uneven use of transitional strategies, with little variety • weak or uneven sequence of events • weak opening and closing	• **uneven** elaboration with **partial** details, dialogue, description • uneven expression of experiences and events • vague, abrupt, or imprecise use of source material • uneven, inconsistent use of narrative technique • partial or weak use of sensory, concrete, and figurative language	• **adequate** command of spelling, capitalization, punctuation, grammar, and usage • few errors
1	• **basic** organization; **little or no** focus • little or no discernible plot; may just be a series of events • brief or no development of setting, characters, point of view • few or no transitional strategies • little or no organization of event sequence; extraneous ideas • no opening and/or closing	• **minimal** elaboration with **few or no** details, dialogue, description • confusing expression of experiences and events • little or no use of source material • minimal or incorrect use of narrative techniques • little or no use of sensory, concrete, and figurative language	• **partial** command of spelling, capitalization, punctuation, grammar, and usage • some patterns of errors

Teacher Introduction

INFORMATIONAL PERFORMANCE TASK SCORING RUBRIC

Score	Purpose/Organization	Evidence/Elaboration	Conventions
4	• **effective** organizational structure • clear statement of main idea based on purpose, audience, task • consistent use of various transitions • logical progression of ideas	• **convincing** support for main idea; **effective** use of sources • integrates comprehensive evidence from sources • relevant references • effective use of elaboration • audience-appropriate domain-specific vocabulary	
3	• **evident** organizational structure • adequate statement of main idea based on purpose, audience, task • adequate, somewhat varied use of transitions • adequate progression of ideas	• **adequate** support for main idea; **adequate** use of sources • some integration of evidence from sources • references may be general • adequate use of some elaboration • generally audience-appropriate domain-specific vocabulary	
2	• **inconsistent** organizational structure • unclear or somewhat unfocused main idea • inconsistent use of transitions with little variety • formulaic or uneven progression of ideas	• **uneven** support for main idea; **limited** use of sources • weakly integrated, vague, or imprecise evidence from sources • references are vague or absent • weak or uneven elaboration • uneven domain-specific vocabulary	• **adequate** command of spelling, capitalization, punctuation, grammar, and usage • few errors
1	• **little or no** organizational structure • few or no transitions • frequent extraneous ideas; may be formulaic • may lack introduction and/or conclusion • confusing or ambiguous focus; may be very brief	• **minimal** support for main idea; **little or no** use of sources • minimal, absent, incorrect, or irrelevant evidence from sources • references are absent or incorrect • minimal, if any, elaboration • limited or ineffective domain-specific vocabulary	• **partial** command of spelling, capitalization, punctuation, grammar, and usage • some patterns of errors

Teacher Introduction

OPINION PERFORMANCE TASK SCORING RUBRIC

Score	Purpose/Organization	Evidence/Elaboration	Conventions
4	• **effective** organizational structure; **sustained** focus • consistent use of various transitions • logical progression of ideas • effective introduction and conclusion • clearly communicated opinion for purpose, audience, task	• **convincing** support/evidence for main idea; **effective** use of sources; **precise** language • comprehensive evidence from sources is integrated • relevant, specific references • effective elaborative techniques • appropriate domain-specific vocabulary for audience, purpose	
3	• **evident** organizational structure; **adequate** focus • adequate use of transitions • adequate progression of ideas • adequate introduction and conclusion • clear opinion, mostly maintained, though loosely • adequate opinion for purpose, audience, task	• **adequate** support/evidence for main idea; **adequate** use of sources; **general** language • some evidence from sources is integrated • general, imprecise references • adequate elaboration • generally appropriate domain-specific vocabulary for audience, purpose	
2	• **inconsistent** organizational structure; **somewhat sustained** focus • inconsistent use of transitions • uneven progression of ideas • introduction or conclusion, if present, may be weak • somewhat unclear or unfocused opinion	• **uneven** support for main idea; **partial** use of sources; **simple** language • evidence from sources is weakly integrated, vague, or imprecise • vague, unclear references • weak or uneven elaboration • uneven or somewhat ineffective use of domain-specific vocabulary for audience, purpose	• **adequate** command of spelling, capitalization, punctuation, grammar, and usage • few errors
1	• **little or no** organizational structure or focus • few or no transitions • frequent extraneous ideas are evident; may be formulaic • introduction and/or conclusion may be missing • confusing opinion	• **minimal** support for main idea; **little or no** use of sources; **vague** language • source material evidence is minimal, incorrect, or irrelevant • references absent or incorrect • minimal, if any, elaboration • limited or ineffective use of domain-specific vocabulary for audience, purpose	• **partial** command of spelling, capitalization, punctuation, grammar, and usage • some patterns of errors

   Unit Assessments

Evaluating Scores

The answer keys have been constructed to provide the information you need to aid your understanding of student performance, as well as individualized instructional and intervention needs.

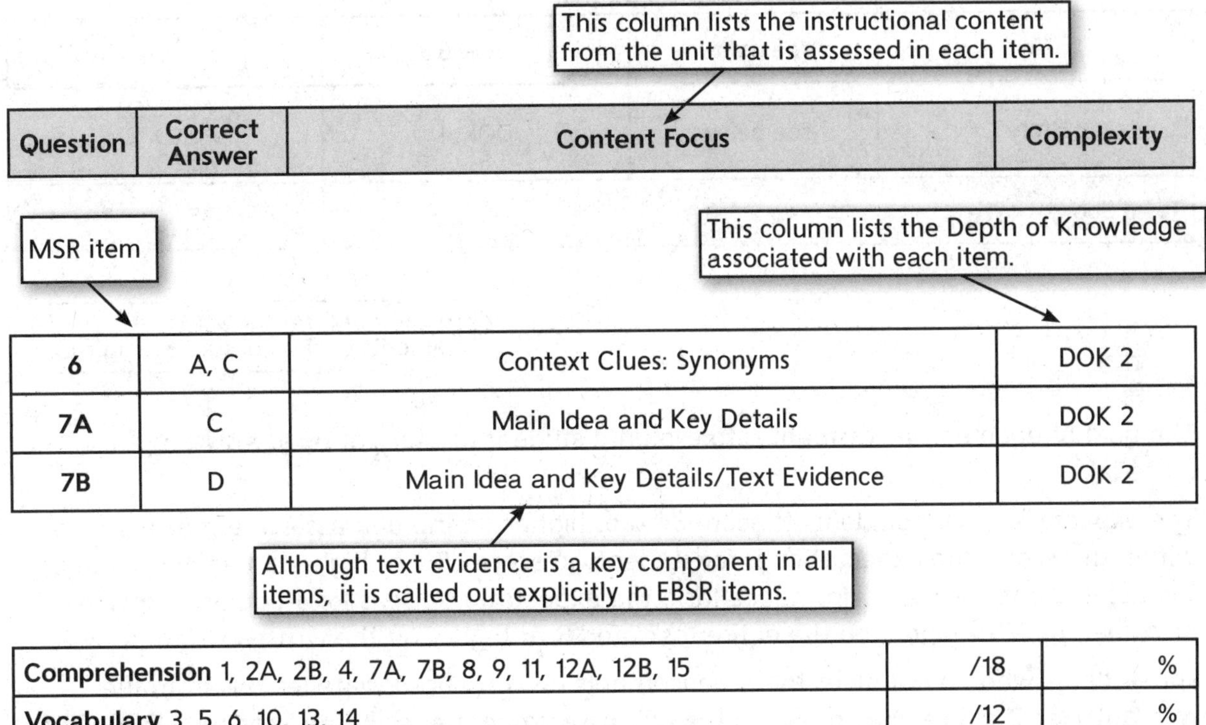

Question	Correct Answer	Content Focus	Complexity
6	A, C	Context Clues: Synonyms	DOK 2
7A	C	Main Idea and Key Details	DOK 2
7B	D	Main Idea and Key Details/Text Evidence	DOK 2

Comprehension 1, 2A, 2B, 4, 7A, 7B, 8, 9, 11, 12A, 12B, 15	/18	%
Vocabulary 3, 5, 6, 10, 13, 14	/12	%
English Language Conventions 16, 17, 18, 19, 20	/5	%
Total Unit 1 Assessment Score	/35	%

Teacher Introduction

Narrative Performance Task			
Question	Answer	Complexity	Score
1	see below	DOK 2	/1
2	see below	DOK 3	/2
3	see below	DOK 3	/2
Story	see below	DOK 4	/4 [P/O] /4 [D/E] /2 [C]
Total Score			/15

This scoring row identifies the elements of the holistic scoring rubric.

The goal of each unit assessment is to evaluate student mastery of previously taught material.

The expectation is for students to score 80% or higher on the unit assessment as a whole; within this score, the expectation is for students to score 75% or higher on each section of the assessment. For the performance task, the expectation also is for students to score 80% or higher, or 12 or higher on the entire task, and 8 or higher on the written response.

For students who do not meet these benchmarks, assign appropriate lessons from the relevant **Tier 2 online PDFs**. Refer to the unit assessment pages in the Teacher's Edition of *Wonders* for specific lessons. For the performance task, the expectation is for students to score 12 or higher on the entire task, and 8 or higher on the written response.

Read the text. Then answer the questions.

Camping Without a Phone

I couldn't believe it when my parents told me we were spending our winter vacation going camping! They are always trying to get me to go outside more. It seems like my mom is constantly saying, "Brian, turn off the computer!" or "Brian, put down your phone and talk to us!" They don't seem to understand that I'm in the zone when I'm using a keyboard, so of course I don't want to stop.

We drove for an hour to Everglades National Park. As soon as we got there, my cell phone stopped working. The precaution I had taken of fully charging it had done no good. I couldn't get a signal for it. Suddenly, I was facing three days of no contact with the outside world. My little brother, Ben, thought it was amusing, and my mom tried to convince me I'd like it. "You'll be able to look around more when you're not staring at a screen," she said.

"You might have to act like a human being," said Ben as he started laughing. Then he escaped to the other side of the campground.

We took a hike with a ranger in the afternoon. At first, I couldn't care less, but after a while I started paying attention. By the end of the hike, I realized there was more action going on in the park than in most video games. It just didn't happen as obviously.

First, the ranger explained that fires can be beneficial for the Everglades. Lightning starts the fires. The pines and some other trees resist fire, and their branches are too high for the fires to reach. Other trees and plants that try to take over from the pines are lower and get burned away. I could almost envision the fires burning around us while we walked, as if they were on a video screen.

Then we stopped to look at a pile of fur and little bones, apparently left behind by a bobcat. They were probably the remains of a rabbit. The ranger said that bobcats hunt nearly every night and sometimes eat animals as large as a deer. Unfortunately, we didn't get to see the action, but we saw some of the results.

Then we saw a wood stork wading and moving its beak back and forth. It was over three feet tall. Because the water is muddy and full of plants, it can't see the small fish it's trying to catch. But its beak is very sensitive. When it touches a fish, its beak snaps closed in 25 milliseconds! That's faster than some computer networks respond when I touch a key.

GO ON →

That night I was exhausted from walking all day, and because I didn't use enough sunscreen I looked a little like what the ranger called the "tourist tree." The gumbo limbo tree has reddish bark that peels off, like it got sunburned. Even so, I woke up in the middle of the night, and I was terrified at first because of some mysterious sounds. But then I recognized the barred owl the ranger had described to us earlier that day. It sounds like it's calling out "Who cooks for you? Who cooks for you?" That helped me to relax, so I was able to fall back to sleep.

We spent a lot of time exploring over the next two days. I started to understand the connection between the land and water and animals. In the Everglades, you couldn't even get rid of the mosquitoes without creating a big change for other animals. Small fish eat mosquito eggs; other fish eat the smaller fish; large fish called gars eat those fish; and alligators eat the gars. If you eliminated the mosquitoes, you might lose some of the other animals higher up the food chain too.

After we left, we talked in the car about the Everglades and how different it was from where we lived. Suddenly, right in the middle of our discussion, I heard a familiar tone from my phone. My friend Jeff was sending me a text. Without thinking, I reached for my phone, but then I put it back down.

"Aren't you going to text back?" asked Ben.

"I will in a little while," I said. Ben looked stunned. My dad and mom looked at each other and just smiled.

GO ON →

1 Put the story events in the correct sequence by numbering them 1 to 5.

____ The family begins hiking with a ranger.

____ The bobcat hunts the rabbit that Brian's family sees.

____ Brian concludes that the park has more action than most video games.

____ The family observes a wood stork.

____ The family looks at a rabbit carcass.

2 Read the sentence from the text.

The precaution I had taken of fully charging it had done no good.

The Latin prefix *pre-* means "before." What does the word precaution mean?

A a warning

B care taken ahead of time

C hard work

D a plan made many times

GO ON →

3   The following question has two parts. First, answer part A. Then, answer part B.

Part A: Read the sentence from the text.

I could almost <u>envision</u> the fires burning around us while we walked, as if they were on a video screen.

What does the word <u>envision</u> mean?

A   hear

B   feel

C   see

D   smell

Part B: Which phrase from the sentence **best** supports your answer in part A?

A   "could almost"

B   "fires burning around us"

C   "while we walked"

D   "video screen"

4   What happens first after Brian wakes up in the middle of the night?

A   He falls back asleep.

B   He hears mysterious sounds.

C   He notices his sunburn.

D   He identifies the sound of an owl.

GO ON →

5 Read the paragraphs from the text.

After we left, we talked in the car about the Everglades and how different it was from where we lived. Suddenly, right in the middle of our discussion, I heard a familiar tone from my phone. My friend Jeff was sending me a text. Without thinking, I reached for my phone, but then I put it back down.

"Aren't you going to text back?" asked Ben.

"I will in a little while," I said. Ben looked stunned. My dad and mom looked at each other and just smiled.

Why do Brian's parents smile at each other? Support your answer with details from the text.

____

____

____

____

____

____

GO ON →

Read the text. Then answer the questions.

Fulton's Triumph

A nervous crowd moved about on a dock on the East River in New York City on August 17, 1807. Robert Fulton was set to make a journey up the Hudson River to Albany and had chosen several brave friends to go with him. It would be the first trip of its kind on a boat powered by a steam engine.

When the boat was being built, Fulton often noticed people making fun of it and joking about it. The boat was big—about 150 feet long—but it didn't look like other ships of the time. It was only thirteen feet wide, and it had just one small sail and a flat bottom. A large paddle wheel stuck out on both sides. People thought it was misnamed the *North River* and should have been called *Fulton's Folly* because it was so foolish.

When it was time to begin the trip, Fulton's friends looked worried. Things did not get better when the *North River* stopped moving only a short way from the dock. Some of the passengers grumbled and wished they had not come.

Fulton was able to fix the problem with a minor adjustment. Soon the boat was rapidly moving up the river. It made its first stop at the town of Clermont. Later, people gave the boat the name of the town, *Clermont*. It traveled the first 110 miles in just 24 hours. Fulton reported passing many schooners so quickly that they seemed as if they were anchored. In another eight hours, the boat arrived in Albany.

The passengers gladly left the boat for dry land. They were thankful they had made it safely. Still, they told Fulton he probably couldn't do it again. Even if he could, they thought it would be unimportant to people.

Fulton posted a sign seeking passengers for the return trip to New York. He would charge $3, the same price as the sailing ships. Only two passengers signed up. Most people were afraid the steam boiler would explode. The crew fed a roaring fire with pine logs. The tall chimney spouted a dense stream of black smoke and a steady shower of sparks. One observer thought the boat looked like a sawmill mounted on a flat-bottomed boat and set on fire.

The steamboat looked very different from the silent, majestic sailing ships of the time, especially at night. The crews of some sailing ships thought it was a monster racing down the river. They hid below the deck when it passed. Other people stood on the banks, waving handkerchiefs and cheering in celebration.

GO ON →

Fulton and his passengers arrived back in New York City safely. The boat had covered 300 miles in sixty-two hours, a little more than two-and-a-half days.

Sailing ships traveled the same route in about seven days. Gradually, people became less frightened, and Fulton's business grew. People were willing to pay high prices for the quick trip on the Hudson. Land travel was slow and uncomfortable. The shifting winds and tides made sailing the river unpredictable. Within a year, Fulton's company was earning $1,000 a week, and Fulton soon became one of the richest people in the country.

Fulton and others improved the design of the steamboats and made them more comfortable for passengers. One steamboat towed barges that contained sleeping rooms. Before, people had slept above the boilers. With this new boat, passengers could sleep well away from the dangers of the fire.

Within fifteen years of Fulton's first voyage, at least sixty-nine steamboats were churning up and down the Mississippi and Ohio Rivers. About fifteen years after that, new steamships were designed to undertake ocean voyages. Fulton did not invent the steamboat, but he made it an economic success. Today, his first boat might be called *Fulton's Triumph* rather than *Fulton's Folly*.

A reproduction of the *Clermont,* built in 1909

GO ON →

6 Read the paragraph from the text.

A nervous crowd moved about on a dock on the East River in New York City on August 17, 1807. Robert Fulton was set to make a journey up the Hudson River to Albany and had chosen several brave friends to go with him. It would be the first trip of its kind on a boat powered by a steam engine.

Write the correct definitions of the homographs <u>trip</u> and <u>kind</u> as they are used in the paragraph. Choose from the definitions listed in the box below. Write your answers in the chart.

Homograph	Definition
trip	
kind	

Definitions:
friendly or generous
a stumble or fall
a journey
a device that activates a mechanism
a group of things in the same category

GO ON →

7 Read the paragraph from the text.

Fulton posted a sign seeking passengers for the return trip to New York. He would charge $3, the same price as the sailing ships. Only two passengers signed up. Most people were afraid the steam boiler would explode. The crew fed a roaring fire with pine logs. The tall chimney spouted a dense stream of black smoke and a steady shower of sparks. One observer thought the boat looked like a sawmill mounted on a flat-bottomed boat and set on fire.

Why did the author **most likely** include this information?

A   to explain why Fulton decided to charge the same price as sailboats

B   to explain why people were hesitant to travel on Fulton's boat

C   to explain how steam engines worked in the early 1800s

D   to explain how consumers felt about the prices of riverboat travel

8 The following question has two parts. First, answer part A. Then, answer part B.

Part A: Read the sentence from the text.

The shifting winds and tides made sailing the river <u>unpredictable</u>.

What is the meaning of the word <u>unpredictable</u> in the sentence?

A   extremely dangerous

B   exhausting

C   relaxing

D   difficult to guess

Part B: Which word from the sentence **best** helps explain the meaning of <u>unpredictable</u>?

A   "shifting"

B   "winds"

C   "tides"

D   "river"

GO ON →

9   The following question has two parts. First, answer part A. Then, answer part B.

Part A: Which statement **best** describes the author's point of view about Fulton's work?

A   His boats were economically successful but unsafe.

B   His bold ideas helped popularize steamboat travel.

C   His inventions were among the most important of the 1800s.

D   His company was more interested in making money than public service.

Part B: Which sentences from the text **best** support your answer in part A? Select **two** options.

A   "The tall chimney spouted a dense stream of black smoke and a steady shower of sparks. "

B   "The steamboat looked very different from the silent, majestic sailing ships of the time, especially at night."

C   "The boat had covered 300 miles in sixty-two hours, a little more than two-and-a-half days."

D   "About fifteen years after that, new steamships were designed to undertake ocean voyages."

E   "Fulton did not invent the steamboat, but he made it an economic success."

F   "Today, his first boat might be called *Fulton's Triumph* rather than *Fulton's Folly.*"

GO ON →

10   Read the paragraph from the text.

Within fifteen years of Fulton's first voyage, at least sixty-nine steamboats were churning up and down the Mississippi and Ohio Rivers. About fifteen years after that, new steamships were designed to undertake ocean voyages. Fulton did not invent the steamboat, but he made it an economic success. Today, his first boat might be called *Fulton's Triumph* rather than *Fulton's Folly*.

How does this paragraph best show that the text is a secondary source?

A   by using numbers to give readers an idea of the scope of Fulton's business

B   by including first-person reactions to the success of Fulton's early voyages

C   by referring to events that happened years after the main action of the text

D   by providing an eyewitness opinion of why Fulton's boat should be renamed

GO ON →

Read the text. Then answer the questions.

Getting Bottled Water Out of Schools

There is no place for bottled water in most U.S. schools. At the beginning of each school year, every student should be assigned a reusable personal water bottle. These water bottles can travel with students to gym class, the cafeteria, and so on. Students can fill their bottles with tap water fountains and quench their thirst anytime. This practice will make American schools greener and healthier. How?

Health and Water

First, water is healthy. With constant access to water at school, students are less likely to pack sugary beverages such as soft drinks and juice. Second, tap water is healthy. Studies show that bottled water is no healthier than tap water. Unless tests show that a school's tap water contains lead, students can hydrate healthfully.

Reducing Plastic Waste

Americans buy enormous amounts of bottled water each year. That number has increased greatly over time. Each additional gallon purchased means more energy spent to transport water, more plastic bottles produced, more energy spent on recycling, and more landfill space taken.

Reducing Water Waste

Think of all the partially full water bottles that people throw away. This is a waste of both plastic and water. With permanent personal water bottles, students will not waste water in this way. They will drink what they want, close the bottle, and keep it. It's all benefit with no waste.

GO ON →

So, schools and students, what are you waiting for? Stop the plague of plastic!

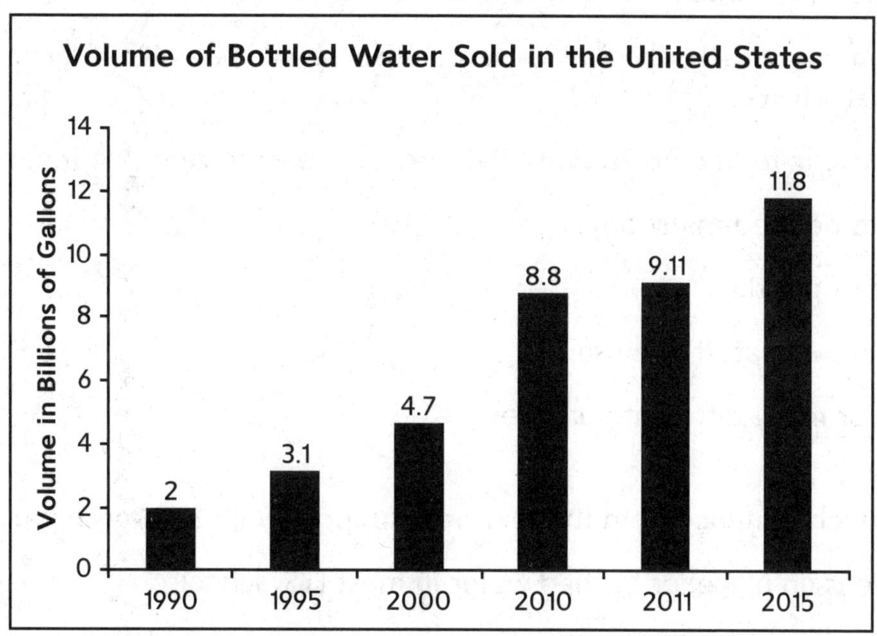

GO ON →

11 The following question has two parts. First, answer part A. Then, answer part B.

Part A: Read the sentence from the text.

At the beginning of each school year, every student should be assigned a <u>reusable</u> personal water bottle.

The Latin prefix *re-* means "again." What does the word <u>reusable</u> mean?

A able to be used many times

B made of plastic

C thrown away after one use

D used for many different purposes

Part B: Which sentence from the text **best** supports your answer in part A?

A "There is no place for bottled water in most U.S. schools."

B "First, water is healthy."

C "Americans buy enormous amounts of bottled water each year."

D "It's all benefit with no waste."

12 Why is the first paragraph important to the author's argument?

A It introduces the claim that personal water bottles will make schools greener and healthier.

B It explains that tap water is just as healthy as bottled water.

C It details how personal water bottles will make schools greener and healthier.

D It presents three main areas in which personal water bottles will help the environment.

GO ON →

13   Read the sentence from the text.

Unless tests show that a school's tap water contains lead, students can hydrate healthfully.

Which word from the sentence is a homograph of a word that means "to be in charge or command of"?

A   "show"

B   "tap"

C   "lead"

D   "can"

14   The following question has two parts. First, answer part A. Then, answer part B.

Part A: Which statement **best** explains how the graph supports the author's argument?

A   It shows that tap water is usually just as healthy as bottled water.

B   It shows that there is not enough space left in landfills to bury bottled water waste.

C   It shows that Americans care more about convenience than drinking healthy water.

D   It shows that Americans are producing more plastic waste from bottled water each year.

Part B: Which sentence from the text **best** supports your answer in part A?

A   "With constant access to water at school, students are less likely to pack sugary beverages such as soft drinks and juice."

B   "Studies show that bottled water is no healthier than tap water."

C   "That number has increased greatly over time."

D   "With permanent personal water bottles, students will not waste water in this way."

GO ON →

15   Use the information in the text to complete the cause-effect chart. Mark **one** box next to **each** cause.

	Effect: Students will bring fewer soft drinks and juice to school.	Effect: Resources such as energy and landfill space are being stretched.	Effect: Students will minimize water waste in their schools.
Cause: Students know they have constant access to tap water at school.	☐	☐	☐
Cause: Americans are buying more and more bottled water every year.	☐	☐	☐
Cause: Students have no reason to throw away water because they keep their personal bottles with them.	☐	☐	☐

GO ON →

The text below needs revision. Read the text. Then answer the questions.

(1) Grandma's eightieth birthday was coming up Mom had asked me to decorate and set the dinner table. (2) It felt like such an intimidating responsibility that I started thinking about it two weeks ahead of time! (3) I wanted her big day to be perfect.

(4) It was easy to choose a theme for the table. (5) For as long as I could remember, Grandma had been a gardener. (6) Her favorite flowers were dahlias, which she taught me how to grow. (7) Dahlias take a lot of work. (8) You have to dig them up before winter, store them inside, and plant them again when the weather gets warmer. (9) The extra work was what made Grandma love them so much. (10) Anyway, I decided that the theme would be flowers.

(11) For the centerpiece, I made a bouquet of dahlias out of tissue paper. (12) I colored them with markers. (13) The plates were easy: Mom had special dinnerware with a floral pattern. (14) I thought about napkins for a long time. (15) I could not come up with something magnificent. (16) Fortunately, the next day was a turning point. (17) When Mom, and I, went shopping we passed a gift shop featuring origami flowers in the window. (18) "Bingo!" I thought. (19) Back at home, I found my origami supplies and made lilies with stiff paper napkins.

(20) The final touch was a flower-inspired accessory for the birthday girl: a crown that I crafted out of real tulips, colorful daisies and ivy. (21) At that point I knew my work was done. (22) No matter how the food tasted or what the weather decided to do, Grandma would have a perfect birthday.

GO ON →

16   What is the **best** way to write sentence 1?

    A   Grandma's eightieth birthday was coming up, Mom had asked me to decorate and set the dinner table.

    B   Grandma's eightieth birthday was coming up, Mom had asked me to decorate, and set the dinner table.

    C   Grandma's eightieth birthday was coming up, and Mom had asked me to decorate and set the dinner table.

    D   Grandma's eightieth birthday was coming up, but Mom had asked me to decorate and set the dinner table.

17   Which sentence has a compound predicate?

    A   Sentence 11

    B   Sentence 13

    C   Sentence 16

    D   Sentence 19

18   What is the **best** way to combine sentences 14 and 15?

    A   I thought about napkins for a long time I could not come up with something magnificent.

    B   I thought about napkins for a long time, and I could not come up with something magnificent.

    C   I thought about napkins for a long time, so I could not come up with something magnificent.

    D   I thought about napkins for a long time, but I could not come up with something magnificent.

GO ON →

19   What is the **best** way to write sentence 17?

    A   When Mom and I went shopping, we passed a gift shop featuring origami flowers in the window.

    B   When Mom went shopping, I went shopping too, and we passed a gift shop featuring origami flowers in the window.

    C   Mom went shopping and I went shopping too; we passed a gift shop featuring origami flowers in the window!

    D   Mom went shopping; I went shopping too, and we passed a gift shop featuring origami flowers in the window.

20   What is the **best** way to write sentence 20?

    A   The final touch was a flower-inspired accessory for the birthday girl, a crown that I crafted out of real tulips, colorful daisies and ivy.

    B   The final touch was a flower-inspired accessory for the birthday girl. A crown that I crafted out of real tulips, colorful daisies and ivy.

    C   The final touch was a flower-inspired accessory for the birthday girl: a crown that I crafted out of real tulips, colorful daisies, and ivy.

    D   The final touch was a flower-inspired accessory for the birthday girl; a crown that I crafted out of real tulips, colorful, daisies and ivy.

Narrative Performance Task

Task:

Your class has been learning about how challenges can bring out the best in people. Now your school is having a writing competition. Each student in your school is going write a story to submit to the principal about their idea for a monument that will honor a local hero. Before you begin to work on your story, you will do some research and find two articles that provide information about famous artists who carved monuments in the side of mountains.

After you have reviewed these sources, you will answer some questions about them. Briefly scan the sources and the three questions that follow. Then go back and read the sources carefully to gain the information you will need to answer the questions and finalize your research. You may take notes on the information you find in the sources as you read. Your notes will be available to you as you answer the questions.

Directions for Part 1

You will now examine several sources. You can re-examine any of the sources as often as you like.

Research Questions:

After examining the sources, use the remaining time in Part 1 to answer three questions about them. Your answers to these questions will be scored. Also, your answers will help you think about the research sources you have read and viewed, which should help you write your story. You may look at your notes when you think it would be helpful.

GO ON →

Source #1: The Making of a Monument

The idea of a mountain monument began as a way to attract tourists. According to the United States Department of the Interior, in 1923 Doane Robinson suggested that South Dakota create giant statues of explorers and Native American leaders in the Black Hills. Robinson wanted lots of visitors to come and spend their money at the businesses in his state.

An Artist's Vision

Robinson contacted the well-known artist Gutzon Borglum. Borglum read Robinson's letter with keen interest; the thought of constructing enormous stone figures fascinated him.

Before long, Borglum visited Robinson and toured the Black Hills. However, he did not care for the needle-like peaks that Robinson suggested for the statues. Borglum thought the tall spires would look like carved totem poles. Instead, Mount Rushmore offered a solid granite wall; it was the perfect carving block.

Borglum also selected his own figures to carve. He chose presidents who had notably shaped the nation's history. The foremost position would go to George Washington; people considered the first president to be the "Father of the Nation." Next on Borglum's list was Thomas Jefferson. Jefferson was responsible for much of our country's growth because he signed the Louisiana Purchase. This agreement bought American land from France, which then owned a large section of our country. Borglum chose Lincoln, too. Lincoln held the country together during the Civil War. For the last position, Borglum decided upon Theodore Roosevelt. This president built our navy and strengthened our country's powers. In addition, Roosevelt was his personal friend.

Finding Funding

Before the project began, a committee formed to find funding. While some people donated money, the amount was too little. Fortunately, Borglum persuaded President Coolidge to visit Mount Rushmore and explained his plan to him. Coolidge approved. As a result, the government agreed to pay most of the costs for workers, supplies, and tools.

GO ON →

Following a Model

How does someone begin chiseling a 60-foot-high head into a granite mountain? First, Borglum built a plaster model of the presidents. Using his model, he measured key distances, such as the width of an eye. Then he multiplied each inch by 12 feet. For instance, a one-inch eye on the model equaled a 12-foot eye on the mountain. Next, workers strapped themselves onto board-like *bosun* chairs. Carefully, ropes lowered the chairs and workers into the correct position on the cliff's face. Then the workers marked the important measurements with red paint.

Dynamite and Jackhammers

Using the paint for guidance, Borglum directed the workers to put charges of dynamite in the places where he wanted some stone removed. Amazingly, he was an expert at determining how much explosive to use to blast away certain areas. After the blasting, ropes lowered drillers with jackhammers. They made lots of shallow holes very close together in the top layer of rock. This "honeycombing" process weakened the rock, so they could take off smaller amounts by hand. Finally, workers used a spinning tool to polish the surface. The different jobs were dangerous, but the National Park Service reports no one was ever seriously injured. After 14 years, the one million dollar project was completed.

A Popular Wonder

Today, nearly three million people visit Mount Rushmore every year. However, the statues are much more than a tourist attraction. People who proudly view the presidential monument consider it to be a lasting memorial to our nation.

NPS Photo

GO ON →

Source #2: A Story Told in Stone

Some Sioux chiefs met and discussed an important idea. They wanted everyone to know their people had "great heroes." They decided to create a statue that would be a lasting symbol of their people's spirit.

Honoring a Warrior and a People

One chief, Henry Standing Bear, wrote a letter to the sculptor, Korczak Ziolkowski. The sculptor's artwork had won a prize at the World Fair and impressed him. Standing Bear asked him if he would construct a large sculpture of their brave Native American leader Crazy Horse on Thunderhead Mountain. Crazy Horse had fought for his people's rights and tried to preserve their way of life. The chiefs felt his courage and bravery represented the Sioux people well.

One Man's Mission

Ziolkowski agreed to the request. He arrived in the Black Hills in 1947 and met Standing Bear. The sculptor suggested carving Crazy Horse riding his horse with his arm extended. His finger would point at the lands where his people once lived. He wanted his masterpiece to relate the story of the Sioux nation.

To pay for the project, Ziolkowski collected donations. While the government offered grants, he turned them down. He did not believe the government would provide enough money to complete the project, and he feared government control of his work.

Carving Thunderhead Mountain

After creating a model, Ziolkowski next determined how to fit his design into Thunderhead Mountain. He began his carving with an explosion that blasted away ten tons of rock. He marked key points and used dynamite to remove unwanted stone.

However, Ziolkowski's work progressed very slowly. The large size of the statue required removing large amounts of rock. In addition, the mountain's high iron content made carving difficult. Also, at first, he had little money to pay for workers and depended on volunteers for help. Despite the challenges, he worked on the project until his death at age 74.

GO ON →

Modern Methods

Today, Ziolkowski's son is the foreman of the operation. The completed face of the Sioux warrior now gazing from Thunderhead Mountain measures nearly 90 feet. Following the sculptor's model, crews have spent the last ten years blocking out the horse's head, which will measure 220 feet.

Over time, carving methods have greatly improved. Workers now use laser beams, which reflect off the rock, to provide measurements. Special gel explosives allow accurate blasting, and bulldozers and trucks haul stone from the mountain. Jet torches polish finished surfaces.

Fortunately, the Crazy Horse Memorial Foundation is able to pay for the ongoing work on the expensive, multi-million-dollar statue. The Foundation collects both donations and visitor's fees.

More Than a Memorial

While the developing sculpture attracts the most attention, the Crazy Horse Memorial offers much more. The site is the home of the Indian Museum of North America. Ziolkowski began the museum because he wanted to preserve the Native American past and tell their complete story. The Indian University of North America shares the location, too.

One day, the Crazy Horse Memorial will be the largest sculpture in the world. The proposed height is 563 feet, which is taller than the Great Pyramid. Often, people question when the sculpture will be completed, but the workers are patient. They remember that Ziolkowski always said, "Go slowly, so you do it right."

GO ON →

1   Mark the boxes to show whether the information in Source #1, Source #2, or both sources supports each idea. Mark only **one** box for **each** idea.

	Source #1: The Making of a Monument	Source #2: A Story Told in Stone	Both Sources
Wanted little government control or funding	☐	☐	☐
Federal government was heavily involved in the project	☐	☐	☐
Monument is an important part of this nation's history	☐	☐	☐

GO ON →

2 Both sources discuss methods for carving a statue into a mountain. What does Source #1 explain about these methods that Source #2 does not? Explain why that information is helpful for the reader. Give **two** details from Source #1 to support your explanation.

____

____

____

____

3 Each source explains that the artist wanted his memorial to give a message to those who viewed it. Explain how including this message affected the design of the monuments. Use **one** example from **each** source to support your explanation. For each example, include the source title or number.

____

____

____

____

GO ON →

Directions for Part 2

You will now review your notes and sources, and plan, draft, revise, and edit your story. You may use your notes and refer to the sources. Now read your assignment and the information about how your story will be scored; then begin your work.

Your Assignment:

Your school is having its annual writing contest. This year, the topic is about an imaginary monument being built to honor a local hero. The audience for your story is your principal, and the school board, as well as people in the community. The winning entry will be published in the local paper.

Now you are going to write a story to submit to the principal. For your story, imagine that you are the person who will be creating a monument about a young boy who helped an elderly neighbor. In your story, describe what makes the boy a hero. Then describe what happens as you plan out your design and build it. What are some important decisions you must make? The story should be several paragraphs long.

Writers often do research to add realistic details to the setting, characters, and plot in their stories. When writing your story, find ways to use information and details from the sources to improve your story. Make sure you develop your characters, the setting, and the plot. Use details, dialogue, and description where appropriate.

REMEMBER: A well-written story

- is well-organized and stays on topic
- has an introduction and conclusion
- uses details from the sources
- develops ideas fully
- uses clear language
- follows rules of writing (spelling, punctuation, and grammar)

Now begin work on your story. Manage your time carefully so that you can plan, write, revise, and edit the final draft of your story. Write your response on a separate sheet of paper.

Read the text. Then answer the questions.

Janko Raven

a retelling of a Hungarian folktale

Long ago, in a faraway land, there lived a humble couple who had a son named Janko Raven. Janko wanted to improve upon his humble beginnings in life, so he went out to seek his fortune. Early in his journey, he came upon a large field. While crossing it, Janko soon noticed a procession of ants marching along beside him. As he observed them, he saw that an ant had fallen into a steep ditch. Janko was a boy with a kind heart, so he stopped to save the ant from its situation. As a reward for his kindness, the ant gave Janko a whistle. "One good turn deserves another," said the grateful ant. "Blow on this when you need help." Then the ant hurried along to catch up with the rest of its peers.

Janko went along his way and soon entered a forest, where he met an old man. Janko thought this would be a good opportunity to mention his intentions. He told the man that he was seeking work and asked if the man knew of anyone who might have employment available. The man advised, "Cross the forest and the great pasture to reach the sea. There you will find the golden castle of the king, who will employ you." Janko excitedly went on his way.

Janko's journey to the castle continued to be eventful, and he saved the lives of a raven and a fish. Each animal remarked, "One good turn deserves another" and gave Janko an additional whistle.

Finally, Janko arrived at the golden castle, where he offered his service to the king. "You will work for three days," declared the king, "and if you succeed, you will be paid handsomely. If you fail, you will be banished from the land."

Janko thought these terms were severe, but he was desperate to make his fortune. And so, he agreed to them.

For his first task, the king ordered Janko to organize a farmyard. He had to put the millet into separate piles of seeds and straw by dawn. Janko knew he must finish or he would face terrible consequences. Just before the sun rose, he decided to blow his first whistle. Within moments, a massive troop of ants arrived to complete the task!

On the second night, the king put his three daughters under Janko's protection. Later that night, the princesses disappeared. Fearful for their safety, Janko used his second whistle to summon a flock of ravens. Flying on the raven king's back, he rescued the princesses.

GO ON →

Janko's final task was to find the king's golden ring, which was lost at sea. He had one whistle left, and he decided that he must blow it to get the help he needed for such an impossible task. As he blew, thousands of fish suddenly swam out in search of the little treasure. It was not long before the ring was found!

"Janko," said the king, "you have succeeded where all others have failed. As a reward, you have earned half my kingdom and three wagons full of gold."

"Your majesty," responded Janko, "only the gold will I take to gladly share with my family." And so, Janko pulled the wagons homeward. Along the way, he left one wagon with the old man who had advised him earlier. His family lived happily ever after with the remaining treasure.

GO ON →

1 Why does the author use personification in the first paragraph of the text?

   A to enable the ant to express its appreciation

   B to create a main conflict in the story

   C to emphasize Janko's humble beginnings

   D to show that Janko has a kind heart

2 Read the sentence from the text.

   Just before the sun <u>rose</u>, he decided to blow his first whistle.

   What is the meaning of the word <u>rose</u> in the sentence?

   A changed color

   B a fragrant flower

   C moved to a higher position

   D stood up

3 Which sentences from the text **best** support the theme that a reward shared with others leads to greater happiness than a reward used for personal gain? Select **two** options.

   A "Janko wanted to improve upon his humble beginnings in life, so he went out to seek his fortune."

   B "Janko's journey to the castle continued to be eventful, and he saved the lives of a raven and a fish."

   C "He had one whistle left, and he decided that he must blow it to get the help he needed for such an impossible task."

   D "'Janko,' said the king, 'you have succeeded where all others have failed.'"

   E "'Your majesty,' responded Janko, 'only the gold will I take to gladly share with my family.'"

   F "Along the way, he left one wagon with the old man who had advised him earlier."

GO ON →

4 Complete the chart to show how the different aspects of the text's setting influence the plot. For **each** aspect of the setting listed across the top, mark **one** sentence that best explains how it influences the plot.

	kingdom with a castle	forest	set long ago, in a distant land	large field
It creates opportunity for the main character to go on a quest and encounter magic.	☐	☐	☐	☐
It creates opportunity for Janko to meet ants, which help him win his fortune.	☐	☐	☐	☐
It creates opportunity for Janko to meet an old man, a raven, and a fish, which help him win his fortune.	☐	☐	☐	☐
It creates opportunity for Janko to work for a wealthy king and win his fortune.	☐	☐	☐	☐

GO ON →

5 The following question has two parts. First, answer part A. Then, answer part B.

Part A: Which theme is **best** expressed in the text?

A Kindness brings rewards.

B Adventure brings happiness.

C Being in nature brings calm.

D Everyone deserves wealth.

Part B: Which sentence from the text **best** supports your answer in part A?

A "Janko's journey to the castle continued to be eventful, and he saved the lives of a raven and a fish."

B "On the second night, the king put his three daughters under Janko's protection."

C "Janko's final task was to find the king's golden ring, which was lost at sea."

D "Along the way, he left one wagon with the old man who had advised him earlier."

GO ON →

Read the text. Then answer the questions.

How Green Is Greensburg?

Until recently, not many people outside of Kansas had ever heard of the little town of Greensburg (population 1,500). Its main claim to fame was a tourist attraction, the World's Largest Hand-Dug Well. Today, however, the town is known world-wide. Given the town's name, it is fitting that its fame now comes from being "green."

May 4, 2007

Residents of Greensburg didn't consider the potential danger ahead when the weather reports predicted thunderstorms. That doesn't mean residents don't take twisters seriously. When alarm sirens told them that a tornado had actually been spotted nearby, they moved quickly into basements and storm shelters.

At 9:45 p.m., the tornado crashed into Greensburg. It measured about 1.7 miles across, nearly as wide as the entire town. Its swirling winds were moving at more than 200 miles per hour. Like a gigantic, out-of-control bulldozer, the tornado zigzagged through Greensburg. When it finally moved on, it had demolished about 95 percent of the town. Homes, businesses, schools, churches, the hospital—even the trees—were all destroyed or badly damaged. The electricity was out, and water supplies could not be trusted. Even worse, ten people had been killed.

Time Line for Greensburg Tornado

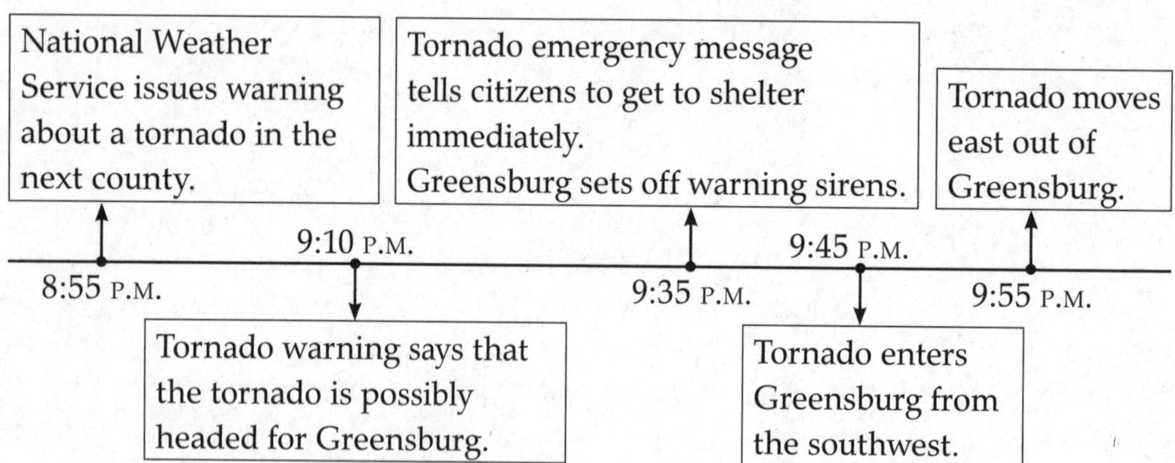

GO ON →

Planning a New Direction

Less than a week after the tornado, the community made the decision that would change Greensburg forever. The people decided that they would rebuild the town green—that is, in ways that were good for the environment. City buildings would use eco-friendly materials and be energy efficient. Citizens would build new homes the same way. Electricity would come from alternative energy sources, such as the wind and sun. Instead of giving up on Greensburg, people got excited about its future.

Building a New Town

Greensburg moved ahead quickly. The first challenge, however, was just keeping the town going. Government helped provide services and housing. A temporary hospital, school, and city-hall were set up.

In October 2009, Greensburg started constructing a wind farm with giant windmills. The wind farm would supply energy for the town. The new county hospital that opened in March 2010 was built to strict LEED standards. (LEED stands for a program called Leadership in Energy and Environmental Design. Its purpose is to support green construction.) The town hall, courthouse, and arts center are also LEED buildings. The new school for grades K through 12 was finished in August 2010. It has natural daytime lighting and other energy-efficient features. Nearly half the homes in town were rebuilt according to green guidelines. Even the streetlights are designed to use less energy and reduce nighttime light pollution.

One of the most exciting parts of the rebuilding is the Chain of Eco-Homes Project. It was launched in early 2009. The plan was to build 12 homes in different designs that demonstrate state-of-the-art green living. The structures would serve as information centers. People would be able to stay in them and experience what an environmentally friendly home is like. The first house was completed in 2010, with construction on others starting soon afterward. Building the Eco-Homes provided much-needed jobs for workers in the area. The unique houses help support a new type of business in Greensburg: eco-tourism. Visitors began traveling to Greensburg to see these interesting homes and other sights on the Green Tour. They brought with them much-needed money and attention. This helped Greensburg continue its unusual comeback.

GO ON →

6   The following question has two parts. First, answer part A. Then, answer part B.

Part A: Read the sentences from the text.

When it finally moved on, it had <u>demolished</u> about 95 percent of the town. Homes, businesses, schools, churches, the hospital—even the trees—were all destroyed or badly damaged.

What does the word <u>demolished</u> mean in the sentences above?

  A   avoided

  B   wrecked

  C   affected

  D   involved

Part B: Which phrase from the sentences **best** hints at the meaning of <u>demolished</u>?

  A   "finally moved on"

  B   "about 95 percent of the town"

  C   "even the trees"

  D   "destroyed or badly damaged"

7   What information does the time line provide about the night of May 4, 2007? Select **two** options.

  A   The tornado measured almost two miles wide.

  B   The people of Greensburg knew only ten minutes in advance that the tornado was coming their way.

  C   The tornado demolished about 95 percent of the town of Greensburg.

  D   The warning signals that were sent out did not reach all the people of Greensburg.

  E   The people of Greensburg first heard about the tornado from the National Weather Service.

  F   The people of Greensburg never received warning that a tornado was coming.

GO ON →

8   Which statement **best** describes how Greensburg recovered from the tornado?

   A   It doubled its population.

   B   It secured itself against future tornadoes.

   C   It became an eco-tourism destination.

   D   It built a new school and hospital.

9   Use the information about word roots to determine the meaning of each underlined word. Choose the meaning of each word from the box below and write it in the chart.

Sentence from Text	Root	Meaning
"Residents of Greensburg didn't consider the <u>potential</u> danger ahead when the weather reports predicted thunderstorms."	*potis*, meaning "powerful, able, capable"	
"City buildings would use eco-friendly materials and be energy <u>efficient</u>."	*fic*, meaning "make, do"	

> **Meanings:**
>
> unnecessary   able to survive a tornado
>
> able to produce with little waste   useful
>
> possible   able to know in advance

GO ON →

10   With determination and hard work, people can overcome difficult challenges.
How do the people of Greensburg, Kansas, illustrate this idea? Use details
from the text to support your response.

____

____

____

____

____

GO ON →

Read the text. Then answer the questions.

The Duel

by Eugene Field

The gingham[1] dog and the calico[2] cat
Side by side on the table sat;
'T was half-past twelve, and (what do you think!)
Nor one nor t' other had slept a wink!
5   The old Dutch clock and the Chinese plate
      Appeared to know as sure as fate
There was going to be a terrible spat.[3]
        (I was n't there; I simply state
        What was told to me by the Chinese plate!)

10   The gingham dog went "Bow-wow-wow!"
And the calico cat replied "Mee-ow!"
The air was littered, an hour or so,
With bits of gingham and calico,
      While the old Dutch clock in the chimney-place
15   Up with its hands before its face,
For it always dreaded a family row![4]
        (Now mind: I'm only telling you
        What the old Dutch clock declares is true!)

The Chinese plate looked very blue,
20   And wailed, "Oh, dear! what shall we do!"
But the gingham dog and the calico cat
Wallowed this way and tumbled that,
      Employing every tooth and claw
      In the awfullest way you ever saw—
25   And, oh! how the gingham and calico flew!
        (Don't fancy I exaggerate—
        I got my news from the Chinese plate!)

---

[1] cotton fabric woven in checks, stripes, or plaids

[2] cotton fabric with a colored pattern

[3, 4] fight

"The Duel" by Eugene Field from *Yale Book of American Verse*. Yale University Press, 1912.

GO ON →

Next morning, where the two had sat
They found no trace of dog or cat;
30 And some folks think unto this day
That burglars stole that pair away!
But the truth about the cat and pup
Is this: they ate each other up!
Now what do you really think of that!
35 *(The old Dutch clock it told me so,*
And that is how I came to know.)

GO ON →

11   The following question has two parts. First, answer part A. Then, answer part B.

Part A: What is a theme in the poem?

    A   Humans should beware of acting like cats and dogs.

    B   We do not always have total control over our actions.

    C   Sometimes the best of friends can turn into enemies.

    D   Secondhand information might not be totally factual.

Part B: Which lines from the poem **best** support your answer in part A?

    A   Lines 1–4

    B   Lines 10–13

    C   Lines 19–22

    D   Lines 30–33

12   Why does the poet **most likely** repeat the words *gingham* and *calico* in lines 13 and 25?

    A   to create a sense of stress and urgency about the fight

    B   to inform readers about the stuffed animals' cloth patterns

    C   to help explain why burglars would steal the animals

    D   to strictly follow the poem's overall rhyming pattern

13   Why does the poet use personification in the poem?

    A   to foreshadow the resolution of the plot

    B   to turn the clock, plate, and stuffed animals into characters

    C   to compare the gingham dog to the calico cat

    D   to create tension between the speaker and the stuffed animals

GO ON →

14 What are **two** important effects of the rhyme scheme of the poem?

   A   It helps emphasize the role of the clock and the plate.

   B   It makes the events in the poem sound more believable.

   C   It helps lighten the mood of a narrative about a fight.

   D   It allows the reader to focus on the most important words.

   E   It helps the reader visualize the setting.

   F   It gives the song a rhythmic, sing-song quality.

15 Match each excerpt from the poem with the answer that best explains how it supports a theme in the poem. Circle the letter next to each correct answer.

Excerpt	How It Supports a Theme
While the old Dutch clock in the chimney-place Up with its hands before its face, For it always dreaded a family row!	**A.** The Dutch clock's reaction shows that it is not affected by the fighting between the gingham dog and calico cat. **B.** A clock always has "hands" on a "face," which suggests that the Dutch clock did not really have such a dramatic reaction.
The Chinese plate looked very blue, And wailed, "Oh, dear! what shall we do!"	**A.** The Chinese plate's emotional response raises the level of drama surrounding the event. **B.** The Chinese plate's emotional response shows that it always acts helpless in difficult situations.
(Don't fancy I exaggerate— *I got my news from the Chinese plate!)*	**A.** By citing the Chinese plate as the source, the speaker proves that he or she is trustworthy. **B.** By having the speaker deny it, the author suggests that the speaker is, in fact, exaggerating.

GO ON →

The text below needs revision. Read the text. Then answer the questions.

(1) Many years ago, chipmunks did not have stripes on their backs as they do now. (2) They were a plain rusty brown all over. (3) This color made it much easier for their enemies to see them. (4) It was very dangerous being a chipmunk in those days.

(5) One morning, a cat caught a chipmunk and carried it into the kitchen. (6) When the cat's owners yelled, the startled cat dropped its prey. (7) Quickly, the chipmunk scooted away and hid behind the woodstove. (8) The peoples were cooking, and the stove was warm. (9) It burned the chipmunk's fur just a little bit. (10) By the time the chipmunk escaped, it had black, gray, and white stripes all down its back.

(11) The chipmunk found that its new colors gave it protection. (12) The stripes looked like bands of shadow and sunlight, making it much easier to hide from predators. (13) Other chipmunks decided they wanted striped coats too. (14) Soon they were finding ways to sneak into the house and visit the woodstove. (15) That's why today chipmunkses' coats all have stripes.

GO ON →

16 What is the prepositional phrase in sentence 1?

  A Many years ago

  B did not have stripes

  C on their backs

  D as they do now

17 What is the purpose of the prepositional phrase in sentence 7?

  A to show how the chipmunk ran

  B to tell where the chipmunk hid

  C to tell where the stove was

  D to describe the stove

18 How can sentence 8 **best** be written?

  A The people's was cooking, and the stove was warm.

  B The peoples' were cooking, and the stove was warm.

  C The people was cooking, and the stove was warm.

  D The people were cooking, and the stove was warm.

19 Which sentence contains an abstract noun?

  A Sentence 9

  B Sentence 10

  C Sentence 11

  D Sentence 13

GO ON →

20 How can sentence 15 **best** be written?

A That's why today chipmunks's coats all have stripes.

B That's why today chipmunks' coats all have stripes.

C That's why today chipmunk's coats all have stripes.

D That's why today chipmunks coats all have stripes.

Informational Performance Task

Task:

Your class has been learning about inventors and how they put their plans into action. Now your school newspaper is creating a special edition about inventions. Your teacher has asked you to write an informational article about the process of turning an idea into an invention. Before you begin, you do some research and find two articles that provide information about famous inventors, and one article about how to get a patent for your invention.

After you have reviewed these sources, you will answer some questions about them. Briefly scan the sources and the three questions that follow. Then go back and read the sources carefully to gain the information you will need to answer the questions and finalize your research. You may take notes on the information you find in the sources as you read. Your notes will be available to you as you answer the questions.

Directions for Part 1

You will now examine several sources. You can re-examine any of the sources as often as you like.

Research Questions:

After examining the sources, use the remaining time in Part 1 to answer three questions about them. Your answers to these questions will be scored. Also, your answers will help you think about the research sources you have read and viewed, which should help you write your informational article.

You may look at your notes when you think it would be helpful.

GO ON →

Source #1: George Nissen

When George Nissen was sixteen years old, he saw something that sparked an invention. George saw a trapeze act at the circus. The trapeze artists would twirl and swing from ropes and swings high in the air, while beneath them was a safety net. Sometimes, the trapeze artists would bounce down onto the safety net on purpose, and then do somersaults. George thought that looked like fun, especially if they could find a way to continue bouncing and performing somersaults. This sparked an idea that would take George on a life-long journey.

George was particularly interested because he enjoyed gymnastics and swimming. The nets reminded him of jumping off a diving board. He decided to take on the challenge of creating something that would allow someone to continuously bounce. In his parents' garage, George's first attempts resulted in a stretched canvas sheet inside a metal frame. Later, in college, George improved his "bouncing rig" with the help of his gymnastics teacher, Larry Griswald. This time, he used a nylon sheet that allowed for better bouncing.

George and two acrobat friends made a traveling show, called the Three Leonardos, that utilized their new bouncing rig. When they were traveling and performing in Mexico, George came up with the name trampoline. *Trampolin* means diving board in Spanish. He just added an *e*.

George thought the trampoline was wonderful. In 1942 he founded a trampoline company and spent years traveling around the world showing off what people can do on trampolines. He held competitions for rebound tumbling, the original name of trampoline competitions. He thought it would be neat if people could compete on trampolines in the Olympics. He invented games, such as Spaceball, a combination between basketball and volleyball. He even rented a kangaroo to bounce with him in Central Park. He sometimes would go to extreme lengths to promote his invention. In 1997, he performed acrobatics atop a flat-top pyramid, in Egypt.

Finally, he got his wish to see trampolines in the Olympics. In the year 2000, trampoline gymnastics became an Olympic sport. George went to watch at the Olympics that year. He was invited to try out the trampoline the athletes would use. He did. He was 86 years old.

GO ON →

Source #2: Chester Greenwood

In the town of Farmington, Maine, the first Saturday of December is Chester Greenwood Day. Residents of the town line the streets to honor a man that developed practical solutions to everyday problems. One idea that made him famous was one that he created when he was only fifteen years old.

Like many inventors, Chester had a problem to solve. Maine winters were cold. People would wrap wool scarves around their heads, but the scarves were scratchy and Chester was allergic to wool. One day, in 1873, Chester had been ice skating and was becoming frustrated because he couldn't protect his ears from the cold. Suddenly he thought of a way to keep them warm: ear muffs. He made a wire frame with two loops that would go over the ears and asked his grandmother to help him sew cloth and beaver fur to the frame.

Chester's family had a lot to do with his creativity and ambition. His father was bridge builder and businessman, and many of the children in the family were creative and mechanical like their father. He, and his siblings, always worked hard to help out around the family farm. Sometimes, Chester would travel several miles to sell fudge and candy that he made himself.

Chester Greenwood is called the inventor of ear muffs. However, he did not really invent them. Ear muffs already existed, but he found a way to make them better. While his first design was immediately popular with his friends and local children, Chester was not satisfied. Like many inventors, Chester decided to make improvements to his design. He replaced the wire with flexible steel. The new material permitted a small hinge to be attached to each ear flap that allowed them to swivel. This prevented the ear flaps from flapping around. The earmuffs could also be folded up to fit neatly in a pocket. Compared to ear muffs that are made today, Chester's ear muffs were not comfortable. However, they were an improvement on what was available at the time.

Chester called his ear muffs "Champion Ear Protectors." On March 13, 1877, he received a patent for his design. He then started a company that made and sold them. He built the company in his hometown of Farmington, Maine, which provided jobs for many people in his community.

Chester went on to invent more than a hundred things that he thought would make people's lives easier. He made a special type of teapot, a machine for working with wood, an improved rake, and many other things. Chester found creative solutions to problems, and the people of Farmington, Maine, have not forgotten him.

GO ON →

Source #3: Getting a Patent

What is a patent?

Let's say you invent something brand new. No one has ever thought of it before, but it is so useful, everyone is going to want one. How can you make and sell your invention and make sure other companies don't make it too? You can apply for a patent. This gives you the legal right to keep other people from using your idea.

What can be patented?

In order for you to patent your invention, it must be a new idea or it must be a big improvement on an old idea. Also, it should be something useful and not be completely obvious. Finally, it needs to be something that the public does not already know about. It is also important to be able to describe your invention clearly and possibly draw a picture or diagram of it. A patent applies to exactly what the inventor describes, so wording is important.

For example, it would be impossible to patent the wheel. Everyone knows about the wheel already. It is not a new idea. However, people patent special types of wheels that they invent to solve specific problems. In order to do this, they need to describe how their inventions are different from a plain wheel and from other special types of wheels. They also need to describe how their inventions work and how they are useful.

How can I find out if my idea is a new one?

Figuring out whether or not you were the first person to think of your invention may be the most difficult part of getting a patent. There are over seven million patented inventions in the United States alone. It is a good idea to search for similar inventions because you will need to show how your invention is unique. The patent office has a special system for organizing inventions to make it easier for people to do searches.

In addition, you should look through journals and books related to your invention. It is possible that someone invented something and wrote about it. Even if it is not patented, it may be considered part of public knowledge. Then, it cannot be patented.

Can I get help filing my patent?

Many people hire patent lawyers to help them research their inventions and file patents. However, this can be expensive, and it is possible to do it yourself. The people who work in the U.S. Patent Office like to help whenever they can, especially when they know someone is filing a patent without the help of a lawyer. Also, there are websites that give good advice on how to go through the process. It is possible for determined inventors to research, describe, and file patents for their inventions themselves.

GO ON →

1   Draw a line to connect **each** detail from Source #2 with **one** statement from
    Source #3 that supports it. Not all details will be used.

Ideas in Source #2	**Details in Source #3**

Ideas in Source #2

The earmuffs Chester patented were an improvement on what was available at the time.

Chester invented his earmuffs to solve a problem.

Chester started a company that made and sold his earmuffs.

Details in Source #3

"A patent applies to exactly what the inventor describes, so wording is important."

"It is a good idea to search for similar inventions because you will need to show how your invention is unique."

"They also need to describe how their inventions work and how they are useful."

"However, people patent special types of wheels that they invent to solve specific problems."

"How can you make and sell your invention and make sure other companies don't make it too? You can apply for a patent."

"In order for you to patent your invention, it must be a new idea or it must be a big improvement on an old idea."

GO ON →

2 Explain how the information about patents in Source #3 would be helpful if it were added to Sources #1 and #2. Use **one** example from Source #1 and **one** example from Source #2 to support your response. For each example, include the source title or number.

3 Explain how an idea can develop into something that can solve a problem. Use **one** example from Source #1 and **one** example from Source #2 to support your explanation. For each example, include the source title or number.

GO ON →

Directions for Part 2

You will now review your notes and sources, and plan, draft, revise, and edit your article. You may use your notes as reference to the sources. Now, read your assignment and the information about how your informational article will be scored; then begin your work.

Your Assignment:

Your school newspaper is creating a special edition about inventors. Your teacher has asked you to write a multi-paragraph informational article explaining how to turn an idea into an invention. The audience for your article will be your classmates, teachers, and the principal. In your article, clearly state your main idea and support your main idea with details using information from what you have read.

Now you are going to write your article to submit to the school newspaper. Your article should include information about developing an idea for an invention. Choose the most important information from all three sources to support your ideas. Then, write an informational article that is several paragraphs long. Clearly organize your article and support your ideas with details from the sources. Use your own words except when quoting directly from the sources. Be sure to give the source title or number when using details from the sources.

REMEMBER: A well-written informational article

- has a clear main idea
- is well organized and stays on topic
- has an introduction and conclusion
- uses transitions
- uses details from the sources to support your main idea
- puts the information from the sources in your own words, except when using direct quotations from the sources
- gives the title or number of the source for the details or facts you included
- develops ideas clearly
- uses clear language
- follows rules of writing (spelling, punctuation, and grammar usage)

Now begin work on your informational article. Manage your time carefully so that you can plan, write, revise, and edit the final draft of your informational article. Write your response on a separate sheet of paper.

Read the text. Then answer the questions.

A Day with Grandpa

As soon as I asked, I knew the answer. All I wanted to do was go with my friend Ethan to watch the new movie that was just released. Unfortunately, my mom had other plans.

"Josh, you see Ethan every day. You need to spend some time with your grandfather," Mom answered with a stern look.

"But, Mom," I whined, "he never wants to do anything interesting." I knew that my grandfather was visiting for only a short time, but I liked adventure, and the things he wanted to do were always a little boring. However, one look at Mom's face, and I knew the discussion was over.

I reluctantly climbed the wooden stairs to my grandfather's room. As I knocked softly on the oak door, I wondered if I could still convince my mom into letting me go to the movies. Much to my astonishment, Grandpa unexpectedly whipped the door open, startling me.

"Hi, Grandpa," I stammered, shuffling my feet. "I was just wondering . . . if you're not busy . . . um . . . . if you'd like to do something together?"

"Sure! Why don't we go for a walk in the woods?" Grandpa exclaimed, grabbing his jacket.

Taking a walk in the woods would be about as much fun as watching paint dry, but I knew I wasn't going to get out of this. I was doomed to spend a lazy afternoon wandering in the woods.

"The woods harbor fascinating secrets," Grandpa started to explain as we walked. "Did you know that you could survive foraging in the woods with only a flashlight and a tin cup?"

I looked up at Grandpa with a puzzled expression, but he just smiled down at me.

Grandpa led the way along a woody path. He moved like a jackrabbit, darting around from place to place to examine the plants that thrived in the brilliant midday sunshine. Stopping at an enormous blackberry bush that ran alongside the path, he began informing me about the plump berries that covered the branches.

Stifling a yawn, I shifted my weight from one foot to the next and tried to look interested. "I know what blackberries are; Mom buys them at the supermarket all the time."

GO ON →

"Sure, you can purchase them at the grocery store, but they taste better in the wild. Did you know their prickly stems can be peeled and consumed, too?" Grandpa asked, as he plucked a few berries off the branches and dropped them into my hands.

As soon as the sweet, delicious berries touched my tongue, my eyes widened. Grandpa was right: they were delicious!

I had to admit, I was starting to get interested. "Are there other plants in the woods that could be eaten?" I asked, my stomach growling.

"Yes, all around you, but not all plants are edible; some are poisonous and could make you sick, or worse."

"This is foxglove," he continued, gesturing to a delicate, bell-shaped flower, "which is used to make something called *digitalis*, a medicine for people with heart disease." Then, in a somber tone, he warned, "If a healthy person ate it, it could make them very sick. Before you eat anything that is unfamiliar, it's very important to ask an adult."

As I cautiously examined the seemingly harmless plant, I began to wonder how Grandpa knew so many interesting things about the woods. "Could we find some more plants?" I asked. Maybe this day would turn out to be an adventure, after all.

GO ON →

1   Read the sentence from the text.

He moved like a jackrabbit, darting around from place to place to examine the plants that thrived in the brilliant midday sunshine.

What does the simile "He moved like a jackrabbit" show about Grandpa?

A   He is confused by his surroundings.

B   He likes to study animals as well as plants.

C   He is enthusiastic about exploring the woods.

D   He finds being in the woods overwhelming.

2   Complete the chart to show how each piece of dialogue reveals a character trait of the speaker. Mark **one** box next to each excerpt.

	has a lot of knowledge	is curious	is dedicated to family	has a desire to be entertained
"Josh, you see Ethan every day. You need to spend some time with your grandfather," Mom answered with a stern look. (Mom)	☐	☐	☐	☐
"But, Mom," I whined, "he never wants to do anything interesting." (Josh)	☐	☐	☐	☐
"This is foxglove . . . which is used to make something called *digitalis,* a medicine for people with heart disease." (Grandpa)	☐	☐	☐	☐
"Could we find some more plants?" I asked. (Josh)	☐	☐	☐	☐

GO ON →

3   The following question has two parts. First, answer part A. Then, answer part B.

Part A: What is a theme in the text?

A   Rebelling against rules can lead to trouble.

B   People have more in common with peers than family.

C   Nature, like life, can be dark and mysterious.

D   Everyone has something special to offer.

Part B: Which excerpt from the text **best** supports your answer in part A?

A   "'But, Mom,' I whined. 'He never wants to do anything interesting.'"

B   "However, one look at Mom's face, and I knew the discussion was over."

C   "'Sure, you can purchase them at the grocery store, but they taste better in the wild.'"

D   "Maybe this day would turn out to be an adventure, after all."

4   Which sentence from the text **best** supports the theme that nature should be treated with respect and caution?

A   "'I know what blackberries are; Mom buys them at the supermarket all the time.'"

B   "'Did you know their prickly stems can be peeled and consumed, too?'"

C   "'This is foxglove . . . which is used to make . . . a medicine for people with heart disease.'"

D   "'If a healthy person ate it, it could make them very sick.'"

GO ON →

5 The following question has two parts. First, answer part A. Then, answer part B.

Part A: Read the excerpt from the text.

I had to admit, I was starting to get interested. "Are there other plants in the woods that could be eaten?" I asked, my stomach growling.

"Yes, all around you, but not all plants are <u>edible</u>; some are poisonous and could make you sick, or worse."

What does the word <u>edible</u> mean?

A   tasty

B   pretty to see

C   safe to eat

D   well known

Part B: Which phrases from the excerpt **best** help you understand the meaning of <u>edible</u>? Select **two** options.

A   "starting to get interested"

B   "could be eaten"

C   "my stomach growling"

D   "all around you"

E   "not all plants"

F   "could make you sick"

GO ON →

Read the text. Then answer the questions.

Tiny Wintry World

Hold the glass globe in your hands and turn it over gently. Then flip it back and watch as snow falls slowly over a tiny village. For kids and grownups everywhere, snow globes hold a special delight. Yet these fun keepsakes actually came to be because of an experiment that did not work.

In 1900, a man named Erwin Perzy was trying to figure out a way to create more light. Perzy lived in Vienna, Austria, and he made tools to be used for surgery. At that time, the electric light bulb had just been invented, but it created inadequate light. A surgeon asked Perzy to come up with a way to make the light brighter for his operating room.

Perzy contemplated the problem carefully. He remembered how shoemakers would use a special trick to get more light from candles. They would place a glass globe full of water in front of the flame. The light would shine through the globe and cast a golden glow about the size of a hand.

With this in mind, Perzy filled a glass globe with water and placed it in front of his electric light. He was not satisfied with how bright it was, so he decided to add to the idea. First, he tried adding glitter to the water. When it first dropped into the water, the glitter reflected the light and added brightness to the room. However, it sank to the bottom, and the shining effect was gone.

Although his first idea had failed, Perzy felt he was onto something. He tried to find a material that weighed even less than the glitter. After searching, he came upon a fine white powder called semolina. It was usually used to make baby food. Perzy thought the powder would be perfect for his light globe, so he dropped it in. Once again, the powder made the light brighter, but it also soon came to rest on the bottom of the globe. Perzy's experiment failed again. However, it sparked a new idea. For to Perzy, the sinking white powder looked just like fresh falling snow.

Fascinated by his new discovery, Perzy decided the snow should fall onto something. He took a soft, silvery metal called pewter, which he had in his workshop, and made a tiny model of a famous building in Austria. Perzy placed the little structure into the globe and watched the "snow" fall on it. He became even more excited—surely other people would enjoy his globes as much as he did! Quickly, Perzy got a patent for his "glass globe with snow effect." The patent would prove that he invented it.

GO ON →

Over the next few years, Perzy experimented with different materials to find the right one for his snow. He also tried different miniature buildings. In 1905, Perzy opened a small factory to make the snow globes and they quickly became popular. The Austrian emperor, Franz Josef I, even gave Perzy a special award for his new toy. Soon, snow globes could be found in homes all around the world, from cottages to the White House.

Today, Perzy's company, Original Vienna Snow Globes, still produces hundreds of thousands of snow globes each year. Each one is handmade. There are more than 2,000 scenes to choose from, including buildings, animals, nature scenes, and characters. Perzy's family has continued his work, and Erwin Perzy III now runs the company.

Erwin Perzy III really enjoys seeing children visit the company and its museum. Even though snow globes do not have batteries, bright lights, or fun noises, kids are fascinated with them. "When the kids come here," he says, "their eyes are wide open, they are enchanted, and everyone has one or two snow globes in their hands, and they are shaking them. That is a very nice moment for me." While his grandfather's experiment long ago did not work, it actually led to something even more wonderful.

GO ON →

6 Which statement **best** represents the author's point of view about Perzy?

  A Perzy was not skilled in using electricity.

  B Perzy was able to learn from his failures.

  C Perzy was not creative enough to be an inventor.

  D Perzy was mainly interested in surgical tools.

7 The following question has two parts. First, answer part A. Then, answer part B.

Part A: Read the sentences from the text.

Perzy <u>contemplated</u> the problem carefully. He remembered how shoemakers would use a special trick to get more light from candles.

What does the word <u>contemplated</u> mean?

  A changed around

  B solved quickly

  C thought about

  D worried over

Part B: Which word from the sentences **best** helps you understand the meaning of <u>contemplated</u>?

  A "remembered"

  B "special"

  C "trick"

  D "candles"

GO ON →

8 Read the sentences from the text.

He took a soft, silvery metal called pewter, which he had in his workshop, and made a tiny model of a famous building in Austria. Perzy placed the little <u>structure</u> into the globe and watched the "snow" fall on it.

Which words from the sentences **best** help to define <u>structure</u>? Select **two** options.

A "metal"

B "pewter"

C "workshop"

D "model"

E "building"

F "snow"

9 Complete the sentences about the main idea of the text. Circle **one** main idea and **one** detail.

The main idea in "Tiny Wintry World" is that __________. This is **best**

supported by the detail __________.

Main Idea	Detail
snow globes made Erwin Perzy famous	"because of an experiment that did not work"
snow globes were discovered accidentally	"even gave Perzy a special award for his new toy"
snow globes can have different kinds of scenes inside	"including buildings, animals, nature scenes, and characters"

GO ON →

10 Why did the author **most likely** choose to write about Erwin Perzy? Support your answer with details from the text.

____

____

____

____

____

____

GO ON →

Read the text. Then answer each question.

Get Those Kids Coding!

Coding is one of the key skills of the twenty-first century. All kids should learn how to code starting in kindergarten. Coding means creating a set of commands that tell a digital machine, such as a computer or a smartphone, what to do. This set of commands is usually called a program, an app, or simply "code." Why should all kids learn how to code? Coding is an essential part of literacy, it prepares kids for future careers, and it is a creative and fun way to express yourself.

First, knowing how to read, write, and understand code is part of the bundle that we call modern literacy, or knowledge. Wherever kids go, they are surrounded by the "language" of code—in their classrooms; at the grocery-store checkout counter; in libraries and museums; and on computers, tablets, televisions, and smartphones at home. Coding literacy enables kids to know and to understand the world around them—and we all know that knowledge is power. Kids who learn how to code sharpen many other skills, such as storytelling, sequencing, designing a product from start to finish, solving problems (called "bugs" in coding language), handling frustration, and teamwork.

Second, kids who learn to code will have a major advantage in their future careers. Coding skills are already necessary credentials for many high-paying and exciting jobs. Even if kids do not want to be computer programmers for a living, knowledge of coding will help qualify them for a surprising number of seemingly unrelated jobs. It can be useful in the fields of art and design, engineering, finance, and health care.

Finally, coding is a wide-open world of personal expression. It's fun. Kids who design and create things tend to be confident, inventive, and enthusiastic. Too often, we interact with technology simply by consuming it—by clicking, skimming a website, or playing a game. This level of interaction does not always require deep thought or even our full attention. Kids who code *make* technology. They get to make the rules for a change! What could be more fun than that?

GO ON →

11   The following question has two parts. First, answer part A. Then, answer part B.

Part A: Which sentence **best** expresses a point of view of the author?

A   Coding can have emotional benefits.

B   Coding is a difficult skill to learn.

C   Coding cannot be taught later in life.

D   Coding is necessary for getting a job.

Part B: Which sentence from the text **best** supports your answer in part A?

A   "All kids should learn how to code starting in kindergarten."

B   "Even if kids do not want to be computer programmers for a living, knowledge of coding will help qualify them for a surprising number of seemingly unrelated jobs."

C   "Kids who design and create things tend to be confident, inventive, and enthusiastic."

D   "Usually we interact with technology by consuming it—by clicking, reading, or playing a game."

12   Read the sentence from the text.

Coding means creating a set of commands that tell a <u>digital</u> machine, such as a computer or a smartphone, what to do.

Which word or phrase from the sentence **best** helps you understand the meaning of <u>digital</u>?

A   "creating"

B   "a set of commands that tell"

C   "computer or a smartphone"

D   "what to do"

GO ON →

13 Complete the diagram with the sentences from the box below to show the main idea and key details of the second paragraph. Not all of the sentences in the box will be used. Write your answers in the diagram.

<table>
<tr><td>Main Idea

</td></tr>
<tr><td>Key Detail

</td></tr>
<tr><td>Key Detail

</td></tr>
<tr><td>Key Detail

</td></tr>
</table>

Sentences:
Coding includes many other helpful skills.
Problems are called "bugs" in coding language.
Coding can be a frustrating activity.
Coding skills are an essential part of modern literacy.
Coding helps kids understand their world and be powerful within it.
The "language" of code is all around kids.

GO ON →

14 Read the sentence from the text.

Coding skills are already necessary <u>credentials</u> for many high-paying and exciting jobs.

The Latin root *cred* means "believe or trust." How would you **best** describe someone applying for a job who has good <u>credentials</u>?

A   someone who is never late to work

B   someone who writes very well

C   someone who is one of the top students

D   someone who seems qualified and responsible

15 Based on information in the text, which **two** problems might learning how to code **best** help solve?

A   our frequently shallow interactions with technology

B   feeling frustrated when facing a challenge

C   the shortage of qualified sales professionals

D   children spending too much time playing video games

E   the common fear of public speaking

F   the steady decline in students reading for pleasure

GO ON →

The text below needs revision. Read the text. Then answer the questions.

(1) Are you planning to stay home and catch up on those comic books this weekend? (2) Think again! (3) We, the editors of *Talk of Thompson*, highly encourage all Thompson Elementary students to attend the Fourth Annual Plant a Tree Day. (4) Below will be three reasons why it's in your best interest to make an extra trek to 55 Juniper Lane this weekend.

(5) Reason 3: Our very own tree-loving teachers, Ms. Frond and Mr. Wonderleaf, will have been on site. (6) This small team of experts have extensive knowledge of all things green and plantlike. (7) Are you curious about why fertilizer helps trees grow? (8) Ms. Frond will break down the ingredients of fertilizer for you! (9) Have you forgotten about the difference between stem and trunk or stamen and pistil? (10) Friendly plant expert Mr. Wonderleaf will refresh your memory!

(11) Reason 2: You can leave your bagged lunches at home because we will be serving a healthy and delectable lunch. (12) That's right—you're eyes are'nt fooling you. (13) Napoli's Pizza is donating all the veggie pies and water coolers we need to keep our planting muscles primed with energy.

(14) Reason 1: At last we arrive at the top reason why you should—no, must—take time out of your weekend schedule to show up at Plant a Tree Day. (15) Ladies and gentlemen, after planting *fifteen* trees on Thompson's grounds, you and your schoolmates will literally breathe easier. (16) It's true: the new trees will provide a higher quantity and quality of air for the citizens of our educational community.

(17) See you there!

GO ON →

16 What is the **best** way to write sentence 4?

A Below, will be three reasons why it's in your best interest to make an extra trek to 55 Juniper Lane this weekend.

B Below are three reasons why it's in your best interest to make an extra trek to 55 Juniper Lane this weekend.

C Below will be three reasons why its in your best interest to make an extra trek to 55 Juniper Lane this weekend.

D Below were three reasons why it's in your best interest to make an extra trek to 55 Juniper Lane this weekend.

17 What is the correct way to write sentence 5?

A Reason 3: Our very own tree-loving teachers, Ms. Frond and Mr. Wonderleaf, are being on site.

B Reason 3: Our very own tree-loving teachers, Ms. Frond and Mr. Wonderleaf, will have being on site.

C Reason 3: Our very own tree-loving teachers, Ms. Frond and Mr. Wonderleaf, will be on site.

D Reason 3: Our very own tree-loving teachers, Ms. Frond and Mr. Wonderleaf, be on site.

18 What is the correct way to write sentence 6?

A This small team of experts has extensive knowledge of all things green and plantlike.

B This small team of expert have extensive knowledge of all things green and plantlike.

C This small teams of expert have extensive knowledge of all things green and plantlike.

D This small teams of experts has extensive knowledge of all things green and plantlike.

GO ON →

19   Which sentence uses a helping verb with a main verb?

   A   Sentence 1

   B   Sentence 3

   C   Sentence 7

   D   Sentence 10

20   What is the correct way to write sentence 12?

   A   That's right—you're eyes aren't fooling you.

   B   That's right—your eyes aren't fooling you.

   C   That's right—your eyes are'nt fooling you.

   D   Thats right—your eyes aren't fooling you.

Opinion Performance Task

Task:

Your class has been learning about bees and their positive and negative aspects. Now your school board has announced that it is considering allowing a local company to donate materials and train the students and staff to raise bees at the school. Your principal has asked students to write a multi-paragraph essay that explains your opinion about the plan to the school board. Before you begin, you do some research and find three articles about bees and beekeeping.

After you have reviewed these sources, you will answer some questions about them. Briefly scan the sources and the three questions that follow. Then go back and review the sources carefully to gain the information you will need to answer the questions and finalize your research. You may take notes on the information you find in the sources as you read. Your notes will be available to you as you answer the questions.

Directions for Part 1

You will now examine several sources. You can reexamine any of the sources as often as you like.

Research Questions:

After examining the sources, use the remaining time in Part I to answer the three questions. Your answers to these questions will be scored. Also, your answers will help you think about the sources you have read, and viewed, which should help you write your opinion essay.

You may look at your notes when you think it would be helpful.

GO ON →

Source #1: A Golden Treasure

In ancient Greece, one wise man thought honey trickled down into the sky from rainbows, and bees gathered the drops from the air. Today, people know bees make honey in their hives. The busy insects must collect nectar from two million flowers to produce one pound of honey. Their hard work gives us a special food.

A Tasty Treasure

For thousands of years, people have valued honey for its sweet flavors. Sometimes, these flavors vary. The taste of the honey depends on the nectar the bees collect. For instance, if the busy bees gather nectar mainly from orange blossoms, the honey is pale yellow and mild. In contrast, honey produced from buckwheat flowers is very dark and strong-tasting.

People have prized honey because it is an easy food to store, too. In fact, scientists digging in Egypt found some honey in a jar in a tomb. The golden food was still fine to eat.

Honey seldom spoils because it consists of little water. As a result, germs cannot easily grow in the syrupy liquid. Sometimes, the lack of water causes the honey to form crystals and turn into a gooey lump. When this happens, the honey remains safe to eat. Warming the jar in some hot water solves the problem.

Super Powers

While people simply enjoy honey's sweet taste, scientists have discovered the food offers other key benefits. One study tested honey samples from various regions in the country. In this way, different kinds of honey, such as clover honey or alfalfa honey, were included. Scientists found that all the honey samples contained certain vitamins and minerals. These vitamins and minerals are an important part of a healthy diet.

Honey also contains a sugar called glucose. Studies show that glucose from honey helps a person's stomach digest and absorb foods. For instance, eating honey increased the amount of calcium a person absorbed by 25%. The body can use this extra calcium for building bones.

GO ON →

Soothing and Healing

Honey has other surprising uses. When a person has a cold, honey works as well as a medicine to stop the cough. In one study, scientists examined 270 children who had ordinary coughs. Some of them took two teaspoonfuls of honey before they went to sleep for the night. Others swallowed a few spoonfuls of sweetened water. The children who ate the honey coughed less and slept more soundly.

In addition, some people use honey to heal minor scrapes. The thick liquid seals the wound and kills germs. The vitamins in honey help the body grow new blood vessels and skin. However, a doctor should always care for serious wounds.

Today, scientists continue to study honey. They are testing whether it can kill germs that cause food poisoning. They are investigating whether it can help people with allergies. Every day, this amazing food grows more valuable. Thank you, bees!

GO ON →

Source #2: Beekeeping for Beginners

A strange squat tower hides behind some bushes in a backyard. Before long, some honeybees disappear inside the structure; it is a hive box for bees. Today, there are beekeepers in every state in America. With the right supplies and some preparation, you can try this popular hobby, too.

Beehive Basics

First, you will need a home for your bees. Usually, beginners purchase a modern hive box. It contains different sections, and each one serves a specific purpose. The base of the box includes the hive stand and bottom board. The hive stand has a slanted front edge that resembles a small slide. Bees loaded with pollen can safely land on the inclined board and creep inside their home.

The top of the hive has both outer and inner covers. The outer cover acts like a lid, neatly fitting over the hive's edges. It protects the hive from stormy weather and gusty winds. The inner cover is a flat board. This barrier prevents bees from attaching their sticky honey to the lid.

In the center of the hive, there are several crate-shaped boxes, or "supers." The bottom super is the brood chamber, where the queen bee lays her eggs. Eventually, they hatch into larvae, which resemble white, curved worms. Next, the larvae grow into pupae, with bodies shaped like bees. Finally, they become adults.

Directly above the brood chamber is the honey super. In this location, the bees construct their honeycomb and fill its waxy cells with honey. Every hive contains one honey super, but you can easily add more.

Special Equipment

Beekeeping does not require many tools, but a few are necessary. One essential object is a smoker. This machine releases little clouds of smoke when pumped. The smoke does not harm the bees, but it causes them to start consuming honey. After their meal, the bees are sleepy, so they are simpler to manage.

You will also need a bee veil, hat, and gloves. These clothing items guard against stings. In addition, some people wear bee suits, but a light-colored shirt and pants work well, too. Most importantly, clothing should always be clean and odor-free. Bees have a remarkable sense of smell, and numerous scents alarm them. If the bees are frightened, they may sting.

GO ON →

Ready for Bees

Most first-time beekeepers order bees for their hive from an established, trusted company. A box will arrive in the mail containing about 10,000 worker bees and one queen. To add them to your hive, you can consult a beekeeping guide and follow its instructions.

Caring for Your Hive

Typically, the bees quickly adjust to their new home and begin their tasks. The queen spends her time laying eggs in the brood chamber, while the workers forage for flowers full of pollen. The bees devote themselves to building a honey supply and strengthening their numbers.

In the summer, you should regularly check on your growing hive. You can add more honey supers if needed and occasionally remove some honey. At times, you should inspect the brood chamber to make sure the queen and the young bees are healthy.

In the winter, your hive needs little maintenance; the bees remain secure inside. However, you must be sure to leave enough honey to sustain the colony during the cold months.

Do you think you would like to try beekeeping? To gather more helpful information, visit a local beekeeper. Most beekeepers are excited to share their experiences and love for their hobby with newcomers.

GO ON →

Source #3: Controlling Problem Honeybees

Honeybees are valuable insects. They produce honey, and they help plants grow by spreading pollen. However, bees near homes can become a nuisance. To control these problem bees, you must understand their behavior and habits. The following information will provide some useful tips to guide you.

Keep Things Clean

Normally, honeybees rely on pollen as their main source of food, but they will eat other available fare. Sweet treats such as juices, sugar, and fruits attract them. In the late summer, when fewer flowers bloom, bees especially seek these easy meals. Because of this, outside dining areas and open trash cans appeal to bees. The key to discouraging the bees is cleanliness. Always line trash cans with bags and shut their lids. After eating outdoors, wash off patio tables and wipe up spills. Close food bags and bring leftover snacks inside.

Recycling bins filled with dirty cans and bottles draw bees, too. You should cover the bins with some type of barrier. If necessary, use an old door screen or window. While the job takes time, it is important to stop the first bees from entering the bins. These bees will share their find with other hive members, and large numbers will soon arrive.

Watch and Wait

In the late spring, you may spy a big swarm of bees on a tree near your home. This happens when a crowded bee colony sends off some bees to start a new hive. The buzzing mass clusters in a temporary resting place such as a branch.

While the swarm looks threatening, these insects are not aggressive. The bees have no hive to defend, so they are not likely to sting. Once their scouts find a suitable location to build their next home, the bees will leave. If possible, the best approach is to be patient for a few days and wait for them to go.

GO ON →

Time for Experts

Unfortunately, sometimes scouting bees select the wall of a building for their new home. They find a way inside through a tiny crack or hole. Slowly, the bees begin to build a hive in the space.

When you notice bees entering a crack on the outside of your house, it is tempting to spray their doorway with bug spray. However, this plan is not wise for several reasons. First, the bee hive may be far inside the wall, and the spray will not reach it. Also, the spray could cause the bees to look for another exit and encourage them to enter your home. Finally, the spray may kill some bees, but their honey will remain in the wall. The sweet food will attract other insect pests.

Instead, you should call a pest control company. They have the proper tools and supplies to deal with defensive bees. Plus, they will remove the contents of the hive.

Once the experts finish their work, make your own repairs. Patch any cracks and plug entrance holes. Wash the area with soap and apply fresh paint. This will get rid of odors, which could attract future bees.

Today, in our country, honeybees help pollinate about 100 food crops. Most often, they are content to search for pollen and will not bother you. With a little understanding, it is easy to live in peace with these beneficial insects.

GO ON →

1   Mark the boxes to show whether the information in Source #1, Source #2, or Source #3 supports each idea. Select only **one** box for **each** idea.

	Source #1: A Golden Treasure	Source #2: Beekeeping for Beginners	Source #3: Controlling Problem Honeybees
The taste and appearance of honey depends on where bees gather nectar.	☐	☐	☐
Bees send out scouts to look for a new place to build a hive.	☐	☐	☐
Queen bees lay their eggs in the brood chamber of the hive.	☐	☐	☐

2   What positive aspects of bees are presented in the sources? Provide specific details from at least **two** sources in your answer. For each example, include the source title or number.

____

____

____

____

____

GO ON →

3 Explain why it is important to protect bees. Give **two** reasons why bees are valuable, **one** from Source #1 and **one** from Source #3. For each reason, include the source title and number.

____

____

____

____

____

____

GO ON →

Directions for Part 2:

You will now review your notes and sources, and plan, draft, revise, and edit your opinion essay. You may use your notes and refer to the sources. Now read your assignment and the information about how your essay will be scored; then begin your work.

Your Assignment:

Your school board is considering allowing a company to donate "beekeeper kits," and train the students and staff to raise bees at the school. Your principal has asked students to write a multi-paragraph essay to give an opinion about the idea. The audience for your essay will be the principal and the school board. In your essay, clearly state your opinion and support your opinion with reasons that are thoroughly developed using information from what you have read.

Now you are going to write your opinion essay to submit to the principal. Your essay should include information supporting your opinion about beekeeping at your school. Choose the most important information from all three sources to support your ideas. Then, write an opinion essay that is several paragraphs long. Clearly organize your essay and support your ideas with details from the sources. Use your own words except when quoting directly from the sources. Be sure to give the source title or number when using details from the sources.

REMEMBER: A well-written opinion essay

- has a clear opinion
- is well-organized and stays on the topic
- has an introduction and a conclusion
- uses transitions
- uses details from the sources to support your opinion
- develops ideas clearly
- uses clear language
- follows rules of writing (spelling, punctuation, and grammar)

Now begin work on your opinion essay. Manage your time carefully so that you can plan, write, revise, and edit the final draft of your opinion essay. Write your response on a separate sheet of paper.

Read the text. Then answer the questions.

The Poet and the General

Characters

NARRATOR

JOHN WHEATLEY: Wealthy merchant, age 58

YOUNG PHILLIS: Girl, age 7

MARY WHEATLEY: John's daughter, age 18

PHILLIS WHEATLEY: woman, age 23

GEORGE WASHINGTON: man, age 44

OFFICER: man, any age

Scene 1

NARRATOR: [*Spotlighted on dark stage.*] In October 1775, early in the Revolutionary War, a young woman named Phillis Wheatley sent a poem to General George Washington. In a letter dated February 28, 1776, Washington invited Wheatley, who lived in Boston, to visit him at his headquarters in nearby Cambridge. She reportedly did so in March 1776, but no one knows for sure. The poet and the general—what might such a meeting have been like?

[*Narrator walks offstage. Light dims.*]

Scene 2

[*The parlor of the Wheatley home in Boston, 1761. Mary Wheatley is sitting and sewing when John Wheatley and Young Phillis enter from the left.*]

JOHN WHEATLEY: Mary, this child has just arrived from Africa aboard Captain Fitch's vessel. I bought her to be a servant and companion to your mother. She speaks no English but seems very intelligent and quick to learn. Perhaps you can teach her?

MARY WHEATLEY: I will happily do so, Father. What is the child's name?

JOHN WHEATLEY: She is called Phillis, after the ship on which she arrived.

MARY WHEATLEY: Phillis. It's a good name. Come with me, Phillis Wheatley.

[*Mary takes the child's hand and leads her from room. Lights dim.*]

GO ON →

Scene 3

[*The dining room of a house, March 1776. General Washington sips a cup of tea and examines some papers on the table. There is a knock at the door.*]

OFFICER: [*From offstage.*] General Washington, Phillis Wheatley has arrived.

[*Phillis Wheatley, now age 23, enters from right. General Washington stands and gestures for her to sit, then takes his seat.*]

WASHINGTON: You are a remarkable woman with a profound gift, Mistress Wheatley. Certainly, you are someone favored by the muses,[1] to whom nature has been generous. I am flattered you have chosen me as the subject of one of your poems, though I would quarrel with the title: "His Excellency George Washington." I am no "Excellency"—just a man serving his country.

WHEATLEY: I meant no offense, sir. The title merely reflects the judgments I hear spoken all around me. Your citizens think very highly of you, General.

WASHINGTON: I wonder what their opinion will be as this war with England continues. They may feel I have led them out of the frying pan into the fire.

WHEATLEY: Sir, all praise is rightly deserved. Your past achievements—your bravery, honesty, manners, intelligence—are well known. They are the reason the people confidently call on you to lead the brave troops who protect us and gain us our freedom from English tyrants.

WASHINGTON: You say the same in your poem. I thank you for those elegant words. How did you come to write poetry? How were you educated?

WHEATLEY: After I learned English, Mary Wheatley taught me to read and write. Since I was 12, I have read English and Latin poets. The Wheatleys have always encouraged me. They even help me publish my poems.

WASHINGTON: Ah, yes, I have seen your book, *Poems on Various Subjects, Religious and Moral.* I understand that yours is only the second book published by a woman from the American colonies. That is quite an achievement for any person so young, and especially one who has lived in enslavement. [*Stands.*] I am honored to have met you, Mistress Wheatley, but I regret I must now return to my work.

WHEATLEY: General, you have many difficult days ahead. When times are hardest, take comfort in the saying that "the hour is darkest before the dawn."

WASHINGTON: You have succeeded in rising above the tyranny of slavery. That gives me great hope in our struggle with the tyranny of England.

---

[1] the powers regarded as inspiring a poet, artist, or thinker

GO ON →

1 Read the sentences from the play.

[Phillis Wheatley, now age 23, enters from right. General Washington stands and gestures for her to sit, then takes his seat.]

Why does the playwright include these stage directions?

A to indicate that the scene is a flashback to Wheatley's childhood

B to set the scene for the meeting between Wheatley and Washington

C to suggest that Washington was a demanding character

D to introduce the audience to the characters of Wheatley and Washington

2 Draw a line to match **each** proverb from the play with its meaning.

Proverb | **Meaning**

the early morning hours are excellent for planning

"out of the frying pan into the fire"

even if you make a mistake, keep trying until you succeed

just when things seem to be at their worst, they get better

going from a difficult situation to an even worse one

"the hour is darkest before the dawn"

getting back up and trying again after failing on the first try

the danger found even in the safest of places

GO ON →

3   The following question has two parts. First, answer part A. Then, answer part B.

Part A: Which statement expresses a main theme of the play?

A   People can succeed even if the odds are against them.

B   Difficult situations can cause people to behave in strange ways.

C   It can be disappointing to meet one's heroes.

D   Trust is an important feature of any friendship.

Part B: Which line from the play **best** supports your answer in part A?

A   "She speaks no English but seems very intelligent and quick to learn."

B   "I am flattered you have chosen me as the subject of one of your poems, though I would quarrel with the title: 'His Excellency George Washington.'"

C   "I understand that yours is only the second book published by a woman from the American colonies."

D   "That gives me great hope in our struggle with the tyranny of England."

4   Read the line from the play.

Certainly, you are someone favored by the muses, to whom nature has been generous.

Washington describes Wheatley as "someone favored by the muses." Select **two** statements that **best** support Washington's description of Wheatley.

A   She was named after a ship.

B   She used flattering words to describe others.

C   She believed Washington would be a great leader.

D   She arrived in America as a small child.

E   She began reading Latin poetry when she was twelve.

F   She published poems while she was an enslaved person.

GO ON →

5   What point of view does Phillis Wheatley express about George Washington in the play? Use examples from the text to explain your answer.

____

____

____

____

____

____

GO ON →

Read the text. Then answer the questions.

Susan B. Anthony: Champion of Equal Rights

Most Americans know Susan B. Anthony's name, but many do not know the long list of ways that she helped improve American society. From fighting against slavery to working toward equal rights, Anthony spent her entire life trying to bring positive change to American society.

Family and Youth

Susan Brownell Anthony was born February 15, 1820, in Adams, Massachusetts. She was one of eight children in a Quaker household. In her youth, Anthony's family taught her that men and women were created equal. The family was also involved in activism, or movements for social change. In these ways and others, Anthony's family influenced the course of her life.

Teacher and Activist

After her early schooling, Anthony became a teacher for about ten years in eastern New York. This is when she became interested in the temperance movement. Temperance was an effort to limit the use of alcohol. To support the movement, Anthony joined a temperance organization and gave speeches on the issue.

In 1849, she returned to her family, who now lived in Rochester, New York. The Anthony family was still involved in fighting for various causes and hosted many meetings. Around this time, Anthony met other important activists, such as Frederick Douglass and William Lloyd Garrison. Douglass and Garrison, as well as Anthony's brothers, inspired her to become active in the anti-slavery, or abolitionist, movement. Anthony delivered many speeches arguing for the end of slavery during a time when many people did not think women should speak publicly.

In 1853, Anthony was not allowed to give a speech at a temperance meeting simply because she was a woman. This experience pushed her to work toward equal rights for women, including suffrage, or the right to vote.

GO ON →

Elizabeth Cady Stanton Partnership

Another important moment of Anthony's life came when she met Elizabeth Cady Stanton. Stanton was a fellow activist and supporter of women's rights. Anthony and Stanton worked together for decades trying to earn equal rights for women. Often, the speeches that Anthony gave were written by Stanton. Together, they founded a temperance society, a women's rights organization, and a newspaper called *The Revolution*.

Later Life and Death

Anthony's later years were spent in support of the causes that she believed in. In 1872, she and a few other women were arrested for voting in an election in Rochester. After a trial, she was found guilty and fined one hundred dollars. However, she refused to pay the fine and was never arrested for it.

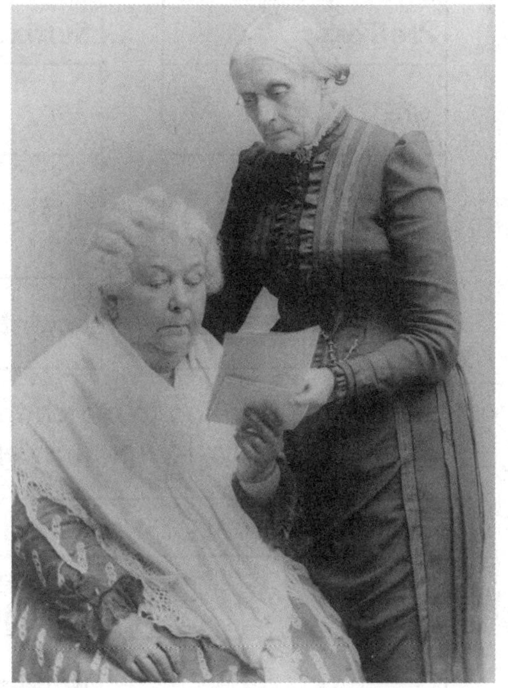

Elizabeth Cady Stanton (left) and Susan B. Anthony (right)

Anthony also traveled around the United States giving speeches for social reform. She fought to change both local and national laws that treated people unfairly. She was active in many groups that worked toward equality. And, she went before Congress every year for nearly forty years to ask them for an equal rights amendment.

Susan B. Anthony died in 1906. Sadly, after a lifetime of tireless work, she never got to see her main goal achieved. In 1920, the Nineteenth Amendment to the U.S. Constitution gave women the right to vote. Because Anthony's work paved the road for the amendment, it was nicknamed the "Anthony Amendment." Indeed, every woman in America can thank Susan B. Anthony for her hard work toward gaining equal rights.

GO ON →

6   Read the following information.

Prefixes	
un-	not
re-	again
in-	in; into

Suffixes	
-er	one who does something
-ist	a person who is an expert in or concerned with something
-ment	the act of

Use this information to match the definitions in the chart below with a word from the text. Write your answers in the chart. Not all words will be used.

Word	Meaning
	a person who campaigns to bring about social change
	to make changes in something to improve it
	a person who encourages someone or something
	in a way that does not follow the principles of equality and justice

Words from Text:

reform	unfairly	amendment
supporter	involved	activist

GO ON →

7 According to the author, what experiences in Anthony's life influenced her to fight for equal rights? Select **three** options.

A She grew up with seven siblings.

B At a young age, her family taught her that all people should be treated equally.

C As a young adult, she was surrounded by other activists in the anti-slavery movement.

D She was not allowed to give a speech simply because she was a woman.

E Elizabeth Cady Stanton wrote most of her speeches for her.

F She refused to pay the fine for voting.

G She also traveled around the country giving speeches for social reform.

8 Read the sentence from the text.

Sadly, after a lifetime of <u>tireless</u> work, she never got to see her main goal achieved.

What is the meaning of the word <u>tireless</u>?

A one who does not get tired

B the state of being tired

C not fully rested

D without losing effort

GO ON →

9   Read the sentence from the text.

Because Anthony's work paved the road for the amendment, it was nicknamed the "Anthony Amendment."

What does the author mean by the phrase "paved the road"?

A   Anthony was the person responsible for getting the amendment passed.

B   Anthony's work in construction gave her a different perspective on equal rights.

C   Anthony asked Congress every year for equal rights, and they eventually agreed.

D   Anthony's hard work helped lead to the amendment's passing.

10   The following question has two parts. First, answer part A. Then, answer part B.

Part A: Which sentence **best** states the author's point of view?

A   Anthony was an American who worked hard to see her dreams come true.

B   Anthony should be remembered for her lifelong effort to improve Americans' lives.

C   With the help of Elizabeth Cady Stanton, Anthony's efforts were finally successful.

D   If she had lived longer, Anthony would have witnessed the progress of women in the country.

Part B: Which sentence from the text **best** supports your answer in part A?

A   "In her youth, Anthony's family taught her that men and women were created equal."

B   "To support the movement, Anthony joined a temperance organization and gave speeches on the issue."

C   "However, she refused to pay the fine and was never arrested for it."

D   "Indeed, every woman in America can thank Susan B. Anthony for her hard work toward gaining equal rights."

GO ON →

Read the text. Then answer the questions.

I Wandered Lonely as a Cloud
by William Wordsworth

I wandered lonely as a cloud
That floats on high o'er vales and hills,
When all at once I saw a crowd,
A host of golden daffodils:
5   Beside the lake, beneath the trees,
Fluttering and dancing in the breeze.

Continuous as the stars that shine
And twinkle on the milky way,
They stretched in never-ending line
10   Along the margin of a bay;
Ten thousand saw I at a glance,
Tossing their heads in sprightly dance.

The waves beside them danced, but they
Outdid the sparkling waves in glee:—
15   A poet could not but be gay[1]
In such a cheerful company;
I gazed—and gazed—but little thought
What wealth the show to me had brought.

For oft, when on my couch I lie
20   In idle or in solemn mood,
They flash upon that inward eye
Which is the bliss of solitude[2];
And then my heart with pleasure fills,
And dances with the daffodils.

---

[1] happy

[2] being alone

"I Wandered Lonely as a Cloud" by William Wordsworth from *Poems Every Child Should Know.*
Doubleday, Doran & Co., Inc., 1904.

GO ON →

11 Read the line from the poem.

I wandered lonely as a cloud

What does this simile tell about the speaker?

A The speaker feels sad until he sees daffodils.

B The speaker is a cloud with thoughts and feelings.

C The speaker feels gloomy on cloudy days.

D The speaker is most comfortable alone.

12 The following question has two parts. First, answer part A. Then, answer part B.

Part A: Which of the following **best** describes a point of view of the speaker?

A The daffodils look joyful blowing in the breeze.

B There are too many daffodils beside the bay.

C The vast lake is overwhelming to look at.

D The daffodils are pretty but unmemorable.

Part B: Which pair of lines from the poem **best** supports your answer in part A?

A "They stretched in never-ending line,
Along the margin of a bay;"

B "Ten thousand saw I at a glance,
Tossing their heads in sprightly dance."

C "The waves beside them danced, but they
Outdid the sparkling waves in glee:—"

D "I gazed—and gazed—but little thought
What wealth the show to me had brought."

GO ON →

  Unit Assessments

13   Read the lines from the poem.

Continuous as the stars that shine
And twinkle on the milky way,

Why does the speaker compare the daffodils to stars? Select **two** options.

A   to show how bright the daffodils shine

B   to show how far away the daffodils are

C   to show that there are many daffodils

D   to show that the daffodils are very little

E   to show that the daffodils flutter like twinkling stars

F   to show that the daffodils can only be seen by moonlight

14   Read the themes at the top of the chart. Then read the details on the left side of the chart. Mark the box or boxes next to each detail to show if it **best** supports Theme 1 or Theme 2.

	THEME 1: Imagination brings us comfort.	THEME 2: Being in nature brings us joy.
The speaker cannot stop looking at the field.	☐	☐
The speaker thinks of the daffodils when he is feeling sad.	☐	☐

GO ON →

15 Read the lines from the poem.

And then my heart with pleasure fills,
And dances with the daffodils.

What does the speaker mean when he says that his heart "dances with the daffodils"?

A He feels like he is with the daffodils again.

B He wishes he were one of the daffodils.

C He sees the daffodils dancing wherever he goes.

D He wants to learn to dance like the daffodils.

GO ON →

The text below needs revision. Read the text. Then answer the questions.

(1) Neil Armstrong was a great American hero who dedicated his life to his country. (2) Armstrong was born in Wapakoneta, Ohio, on August 5, 1930. (3) He and his family moved around a lot in Ohio for his father's work. (4) It finally returned to Wapakoneta in 1944, where they finished high school. (5) Before he was ten, Armstrong took his first airplane ride. (6) He loved it so much that he earned his pilot's license by the time most kids earn they're driver's license.

(7) When the Korean War began, Armstrong left college to fight in the war. (8) He flew fighter planes and was even shot down once. (9) After the war, Armstrong finished college and continued flying airplanes. (10) In the mid-1950s, he moved to California to work as a test pilot for the organization who would become NASA.

(11) In the early 1960s, Armstrong officially joined the astronaut program at NASA. (12) He was part of the Gemini program and completed their first trip to space in 1966 as a pilot on Gemini 8. (13) But it is for his work on the Apollo 11 mission for which he is most famous. (14) During this mission, Armstrong hisself landed the spacecraft safely on the moon and was the first human to step on its surface. (15) He famously said, "That's one small step for man, one giant leap for mankind."

(16) After leaving NASA, Armstrong moved back to Ohio. (17) He held many positions in his later years related to flying, outer space, or technology. (18) Armstrong died on August 25, 2012 in Cincinnati, Ohio, at the age of 82.

GO ON →

16   What is the correct way to write sentence 4?

   A   It finally returned to Wapakoneta in 1944, where Armstrong finished high school.

   B   He finally returned to Wapakoneta in 1944, where they finished high school.

   C   They finally returned to Wapakoneta in 1944, where him finished high school.

   D   They finally returned to Wapakoneta in 1944, where Armstrong finished high school.

17   What is the correct way to write sentence 6?

   A   He loved it so much which he earned his pilot's license by the time most kids earn they're driver's license.

   B   He loved it so much that he earned his pilots license by the time most kids earn they're driver's license.

   C   He loved it so much that he earned his pilot's license by the time most kids earn their driver's license.

   D   He loved it so much that he earned his pilot's license by the time most kids earn there driver's license.

18   What is the correct way to write sentence 10?

   A   In the mid-1950s, he moved to California to work as a test pilot for the organization that would become NASA.

   B   In the mid-1950s, he moved to California to work as a test pilot for the organization whom would become NASA.

   C   In the mid-1950s, he moved to California to work as a test pilot for the organization whose would become NASA.

   D   In the mid-1950s, he moved to California to work as a test pilot for the organization, which would become NASA.

GO ON →

19   What is the correct way to write sentence 12?

   A   He was part of the Gemini program and completed our first trip to space in 1966 as a pilot on Gemini 8.

   B   He was part of the Gemini program and completed his first trip to space in 1966 as a pilot on Gemini 8.

   C   He was part of the Gemini program and completed its first trip to space in 1966 as a pilot on Gemini 8.

   D   He was part of the Gemini program and completed her first trip to space in 1966 as a pilot on Gemini 8

20   What is the correct way to write sentence 14?

   A   During his mission, Armstrong hisself landed the spacecraft safely on the moon and was the first human to step on its surface.

   B   During this mission, Armstrong himself landed the spacecraft safely on the moon and was the first human to step on its surface.

   C   During this mission, Armstrong hisself landed the spacecraft safely on the moon, and was the first human to step on its surface.

   D   During this mission, Armstrong hisself landed the spacecraft safely on the moon and was the first human to step on it's surface.

Narrative Performance Task

Task:

Your class has been learning about language and communication. Now the local newspaper is having a creative writing contest. Your teacher has asked each student in your class to write a narrative story for the contest about how they would communicate with a new student from another country.

Before you begin working on your story, you will do some research by reading two articles about different types of communication. After you have reviewed these sources, you will answer some questions about them. Briefly scan the sources and the three questions that follow. Then go back and read the sources carefully to gain the information you will need to answer the questions and finalize your research. You may take notes on the information you find in the sources as you read. Your notes will be available to you as you read.

Directions for Part 1

You will now examine two sources. You can re-examine any of the sources as often as you like.

Research Questions:

After examining the sources, use the remaining time in Part 1 to answer three questions about them. Your answers to these questions will be scored. Also, your answers will help you think about the information you have read and viewed, which should help you write your story. You may look at your notes when you think it would be helpful. Answer the questions in the spaces provided.

GO ON →

Source #1: A Language of Dots

Ten-year-old Louis Braille felt a shiver of excitement as he rode in the stagecoach. He was on his way to the Royal Institute for Blind Youth in Paris, France. At that time, in 1819, it was the first and only school for blind children like him. Louis eagerly awaited his chance to learn subjects like history, science, and geography. The institute had special books with raised texts he could read with his fingers.

Disappointing Discoveries

Sadly, the institute's large, heavy books were awkward to handle and challenging to decode. Louis had to carefully trace the bumpy outline of each big letter with his finger, one at a time, to read a word. Some of the letters had similar shapes and were difficult to distinguish.

Furthermore, the school's library only contained three volumes. Few companies published the expensive books with raised letters. Louis felt frustrated; he began to search for a better way for blind people to communicate through writing. The ability to read and record information would enable them to be better educated and more independent.

Night Writing

Several years later, a French army captain visited the school. He told students about a code he invented called "night-writing." With his system, soldiers punched a series of raised dots and dashes into cardboard. The different marks stood for the syllables in words. Using the code, he could send brief messages to his soldiers during the night. The soldiers could read them with their fingers, so they did not need to light lanterns that enemies might notice.

In a flash, Louis realized the captain's style of writing would work well for blind people. They could read dots much easier with their fingers than big letters. However, the captain's codes were too long; some of the syllables required twenty dots and took too long to decode. In addition, there were no signs to tell readers when sentences began and ended, which was confusing.

GO ON →

A Cell of Dots

For the next three years, fourteen-year-old Louis devoted himself to perfecting his own "raised dot alphabet." After experimenting, he decided to use a rectangular cell of six dots to form his letters. Different combinations of the dots represented certain letters. For instance, two raised dots at the top of the cell represented the letter "c."

Louis's new alphabet offered definite advantages to "touch" readers. The small cells quickly glided under their fingertips. As a result, they could conveniently slide their hand straight across the page and read more swiftly than before.

Louis's new system also included rules to make sentences easier to interpret. For instance, a dot in the bottom right corner signaled that the next letter was a capital. Plus, Louis designed individual symbols for punctuation marks, so readers could correctly group words.

Helpful Shortcuts

As Louis developed his language, he expanded it to include certain symbols that stood for groups of letters or short words. For instance, there was a specific symbol for "ing" and another specific symbol for the word "and." Other shortcuts, like using the letters "sd" to mean "said," soon became popular, too.

Today, people throughout the world use the Braille alphabet. It includes notations for letters, words, numbers, and musical notes. You may spy the dots in public places, like elevators. Thanks to Louis, people can gain valuable knowledge with the brush of their fingertips.

©Christopher Stubbs/Alamy

GO ON →

Source #2: Talking Leaves for the Cherokee

Sequoyah stared in amazement as his fellow soldiers read their letters from home. The idea of using marks on a paper to communicate with others captivated him. Sequoyah belonged to the Cherokee people, and Native Americans had no written language. When Sequoyah completed his military service, he remembered the white man's "talking leaves."

A Bold Decision

Sequoyah married and had a family, carrying on his mother's business as a trader. Later, he trained himself to be a blacksmith and a silversmith. Because Sequoyah had a lame leg that limited his physical abilities, working as a craftsman suited him.

Whenever possible, Sequoyah devoted his time to his cherished dream; he intended to create a written Cherokee language. Many of his friends and acquaintances thought Sequoyah was foolish. They criticized him for wasting his days, but Sequoyah ignored their comments. He hoped to give the Cherokee a way to communicate their thoughts on paper and to record their nation's history.

The First Attempt

Sequoyah had no experience with any written language, but he understood that the mysterious marks on the soldiers' letters had represented spoken words. At first, Sequoyah started making a different symbol to represent every known Cherokee word, carving the characters into bark with his knife. His collection grew at a furious rate until there were over a thousand characters.

Frustrated, Sequoyah realized his system would not work. People could never memorize that many symbols. However, Sequoyah's efforts were not a complete failure; he became an expert at understanding his musical, flowing language. In the process, he recognized that words contained consonant sounds followed by vowel sounds, or distinct syllables.

GO ON →

A Syllabary

Next, Sequoyah focused his attention on inventing symbols for every syllable sound in his language. Some historical accounts say Sequoyah used the letters and numbers from an old English spelling book as models for his symbols. However, to Sequoyah, the letter "S" was just a snake shape. He did not know that in the English language it represented a hissing sound. In addition, he turned some of the letter symbols upside down or sideways.

Determined, Sequoyah worked tirelessly to perfect and limit the symbols in his syllabary. In the end, he divided the sounds of his language into 85 syllables. Sequoyah felt that people would be able to read, write, and memorize that amount.

A New World Opens

When Sequoyah announced that he had successfully invented a written Cherokee language, people scoffed at him. To prove the truth, Sequoyah convinced an important chief to write a letter to a friend using the syllabary and to seal the message in an envelope. Next, Sequoyah brought the letter to the friend and broke open the wax seal. In front of a doubtful crowd of Cherokee leaders, he handed the letter to his daughter and asked her to read it aloud.

Ahyokah, who had often been her father's assistant, did so without a pause. The Cherokee leaders were stunned and impressed; they wisely understood how valuable the "picture talk" could be to their nation. Before long, the leaders worked to acquire a printing press. In time, their nation printed the first Native American newspaper.

Today, Sequoyah's syllabary remains in active use. In fact, some computer search engines and cell phones have created keyboards with its symbols for their users. The symbols once carved in bark now connect people through wireless technology.

GO ON →

1   Read the paragraph from Source #2.

Whenever possible, Sequoyah devoted his time to his cherished dream; he intended to create a written Cherokee language. Many of his friends and acquaintances thought Sequoyah was foolish. They criticized him for wasting his days, but Sequoyah ignored their comments. He hoped to give the Cherokee a way to communicate their thoughts on paper and to record their nation's history.

How does this information about Sequoyah help the reader understand the work of Louis Braille in Source #1? Select **two** options.

A   Braille wanted to share the story about schools for blind people.

B   Braille wanted an easier way for blind people to be able to read.

C   Braille wished to help the French soldiers share information.

D   Braille invested a lot of time to achieve his goal to help blind people.

E   Braille's raised-dot alphabet was not as effective as raised letters.

F   Braille felt that most people did not understand how to read by touch.

GO ON →

2 Describe how the information in the sources helps the reader better understand the different ways people can communicate. Use **two** details from the sources to support your explanation. For each detail, include the source title or number.

____

____

____

____

____

3 Explain how the sources show the importance of persistence. Give at least **two** reasons, **one** from Source #1 and **one** from Source #2, to support your explanation. For each reason, include the source title or number.

____

____

____

____

____

GO ON →

Directions for Part 2

You will now review your notes and sources, and plan, draft, and edit your narrative story. You may use your notes to refer to the sources.

Now read your assignment and the information about how the story will be scored; then begin your work.

Your Assignment:

The local newspaper is having a writing contest. The topic is about how you would communicate with someone who does not speak your language. The audience for your story is your teacher, the editor of the newspaper, and the community. The winning entry will be published in the local newspaper.

Now, you are going to write a narrative story to submit to your teacher. For your story, imagine a new student has just enrolled in your school. The student is from a foreign country and does not speak any English. Your teacher has asked you to help the student feel welcome by learning how to communicate with the rest of the students. In your story, describe how you develop a way to communicate. The story should be several paragraphs long.

Writers often do research to add realistic details to the setting, characters, and plot in their stories. When writing your story, find ways to incorporate information and details from the sources. Make sure you develop your characters, the setting, and the plot. Use details, dialogue, and description where appropriate.

REMEMBER: A well-written narrative story

- is well-organized and stays on topic
- has an introduction and conclusion
- uses details from the sources
- develops ideas fully
- uses clear language
- follows rules of writing (spelling, punctuation, and grammar)

Now begin work on your narrative story. Manage your time carefully so that you can plan, write, revise, and edit the final draft of your narrative story. Write your response on a separate sheet of paper.

Read the text. Then answer the questions.

A Historic Friendship

Aware that he was a witness to history, Kostas found a good vantage point in the stadium and settled in to watch the first modern Olympic Games. Kostas knew little about the competitors, but he was already practicing to be a future track-and-field Olympian: he was the fastest runner in his school. He couldn't believe how lucky he was to live in Athens, with the eyes of the world upon his country.

"I'm so glad the Olympic Games have been brought back," Kostas thought. "I hope they last for centuries to come."

Kostas felt slightly less lucky when a boy about his age chose a spot on the bleachers right next to him. "My name is Christos," said the boy, "and my father is competing in the 1200-meter swim. If you watch the games with me, you'll know everything about all the athletes, and I'll tell you who's going to win everything because my dad is well-connected. Have you heard about the long jumper from France? He's suffered from a chronic leg injury most of his life. But he appears to be out of the woods now. He claims that the injury is permanently healed and he's going to win six medals."

Christos didn't seem to care whether or not Kostas responded, so Kostas simply nodded politely and let his ears follow the growing roar of the crowd. Craning his neck, he spotted a single marathoner who was just entering the stadium. Jumping to his feet, Kostas cried, "That's Spyridon Louis! Greece is winning the marathon!" The stadium and its spectators exploded in thunderous cheering and applause as Louis crossed the finish line and won the most important Olympic event for his nation. All at once, hats, twigs, and flowers flew through the air.

The cacophony had barely begun to die down when Christos leaned over and said, "Did I mention that my father has been best friends with Spyridon ever since they were kids? My dad used to help him carry water for his family's business. . . ."

Still carried away by the thrill of what he had just seen, Kostas barely heard his companion's boastful ramblings. He considered changing seats, but a move would have been impossible; the spectators were already crowded like sardines both inside and outside the stadium.

GO ON →

But by the time the 1200-meter swimming event arrived, Kostas had warmed up to his stadium mate. "Christos," he said, "would you like to join me to watch your father's event?"

Uncharacteristically, Christos hesitated. "Um. . . ." Christos began, turning bright red. "So, I actually can't go with you to watch my father, because . . . because he isn't actually competing. My dad *is* a swimmer—I promise—but he didn't qualify for the games. I lied about him because I wanted you to like me and think I'm interesting."

Suddenly Kostas knew that he and Christos would end up being good friends. "You know, I'd love to meet your father sometime," Kostas said. "Now, how about that 1200-meter event?"

GO ON →

Unit Assessments

1 Read the sentence from the text.

"He's suffered from a <u>chronic</u> leg injury most of his life."

The Greek root *chron* means "time." What does the word <u>chronic</u> **most likely** mean?

A occurring or beginning in the water

B disappearing quickly with little notice

C difficult to identify or to understand

D happening regularly over a long period

2 Complete the chart to compare and contrast Kostas and Christos. Mark a box or boxes next to each word or phrase to show if it describes Kostas, Christos, or both characters.

	Kostas	Christos
Greek	☐	☐
talkative	☐	☐
humble	☐	☐
boastful	☐	☐
on the quiet side	☐	☐
excited about the Olympics	☐	☐

GO ON →

3   The following question has two parts. First, answer part A. Then, answer part B.

Part A: Read the paragraph from the text.

Kostas felt slightly less lucky when a boy about his age chose a spot on the bleachers right next to him. "My name is Christos," said the boy, "and my father is competing in the 1200-meter swim. If you watch the games with me, you'll know everything about all the athletes, and I'll tell you who's going to win everything because my dad is well-connected. Have you heard about the long jumper from France? He's suffered from a chronic leg injury most of his life. But he appears to be out of the woods now. He claims that the injury is permanently healed and he's going to win six medals."

What is the meaning of the idiom "out of the woods"?

A   out of shape

B   out of difficulty or danger

C   living in a city

D   not being truthful

Part B: Which phrase from the paragraph **best** helps you understand the meaning of the idiom in part A?

A   "long jumper from France"

B   "most of his life"

C   "He claims"

D   "permanently healed"

GO ON →

4   The following question has two parts. First, answer part A. Then, answer part B.

Part A: Read the paragraph from the text.

The <u>cacophony</u> had barely begun to die down when Christos leaned over and said, "Did I mention that my father has been best friends with Spyridon ever since they were kids? My dad used to help him carry water for his family's business. . . ."

The word <u>cacophony</u> comes from the Greek *kakos*, meaning "bad," and *phon*, meaning "sound." What does <u>cacophony</u> refer to in the paragraph?

A   the harsh sound of Kostas's cries

B   the poor performance of some of the athletes

C   the loud sounds of shouting and clapping

D   the mess created by the crowd throwing objects

Part B: Which phrase from the text **best** supports your answer in part A?

A   "exploded in thunderous cheering and applause"

B   "hats, twigs, and flowers flew through the air"

C   "his companion's boastful ramblings"

D   "the spectators were already crowded like sardines"

5   Which of the following describes a **difference** between the marathon finish and the swimming event in the text?

A   The spectators barely participate in the marathon finish, whereas they come alive as the swimming event approaches.

B   The main action in the story takes place at the marathon finish, whereas the swimming event is discussed but not seen.

C   Kostas feels sleepy during the buildup to the marathon finish, but he is energized during the buildup to the swimming event.

D   The stadium is crowded with people for the marathon finish, but not as many spectators come to watch the swimming event.

GO ON →

Read the text. Then answer the questions.

Exploring Mammoth Cave

Mammoth Cave National Park in Kentucky is a popular tourist destination. About 390 miles of connecting passages have been explored there, and scientists estimate there may be 600 more miles to go. The cave has an interesting history that is strongly connected to one family in particular.

Three Young Explorers

In 1838, Franklin Gorin bought the property containing the entrance to the cave. He worked to build a hotel near the entrance and turned over the exploration of the cave to three enslaved African teenagers named Stephen Bishop, Mat Bransford, and Nick Bransford. A doctor named John Croghan bought the land and took ownership of the youths the next year. At one time, Croghan treated patients at a special hospital inside the cave.

The three young men explored the cave with only candles and lanterns for light. They were the first to explore many miles of caves. They gave a name to each new wonder they found. They named passageways, such as Grand Avenue, and rock formations, such as a giant stone column called the Devil's Armchair. A large, open room was named the Church.

When they explored a new area, they often carved their names into a rocky wall. Sometimes they wrote their names on the ceiling using smoke from a candle, and many of these marks still survive. They show that the young men's outlook was similar to that of some modern cave explorers. They were willing to take great risks to discover what others had never seen.

Cave Tours

These young men gave day-long tours to people from all over the world. By exploring and talking with visitors who knew about caves, they became familiar with the geology of the cave. They knew how the cave was formed, and they learned the different types of rocks.

On some tours, visitors had to crawl on their hands and knees through a passage for more than twenty feet. Other tours included a boat ride down an underground river. Tourists had to lie down flat in the boat to pass beneath a low ceiling. The guides delighted in giving visitors a chance to "try the dark," which meant leaving the visitors for a few minutes in the pitch black of the caverns. Soon afterward, they led the visitors to the Star Chamber. When they looked up at the ceiling, it seemed that stars were glittering in a night sky.

GO ON →

The young men showed visitors the strange subterranean fish and shrimp living in the cave's waters. Some were completely white, and most had no eyes. They did not need eyes since there was never any light to help them see. The guides sometimes sold these fish to tourists to earn money.

U.S. National Park Service

Both Nick and Mat stayed near the natural wonder they had explored. They gave tours for many years. The next generations of Bransfords, as well as many other African Americans, gave tours until the 1930s when the U.S. National Park Service took over. The Mammoth Cave National Park officially opened in 1941. Then, in 2006, a fifth-generation member of the Bransford family began to give tours through the caverns. He was following in the footsteps of his ancestors.

Today, the U.S. National Park Service offers many different tours. Some of the tours follow the same routes that Stephen Bishop and the Bransfords took in the 1800s.

Popular Mammoth Cave Tours					
Name	**Highlights**	**Distance**	**Time**	**Elevation Change**	**Difficulty**
Grand Avenue	Snowball Room, Thorpe's Pit, Frozen Niagara	4 miles	4 1/2 hrs.	280 ft.	Strenuous
Historic	Historic entrance, Bottomless Pit, Mammoth Dome	2 miles	2 hrs.	300 ft.	Moderate
Mammoth Passage	Largest rooms, early mining operations	3/4 mile	1 1/4 hrs.	160 ft.	Easy
River Styx	Underground rivers and Lake Lethe	2 1/2 miles	2 1/2 hrs.	360 ft.	Moderate
Star Chamber	Star Chamber, John Croghan's hospital	1 1/2 miles	2 1/2 hrs.	160 ft.	Moderate
Wild Cave	Crawling through caves with headlamps	5 miles	6 hrs.	300 ft.	Very Difficult

GO ON →

6 The following question has two parts. First, answer part A. Then, answer part B.

Part A: The author would **most likely** agree with which statement?

A Going on a tour of Mammoth Cave is a big risk that is worth taking.

B The Star Chamber is the most beautiful spot in the cave.

C Early guides were important to the cave's exploration.

D The National Park Service should not have taken over the tours.

Part B: Which sentence from the text **best** supports your answer in part A?

A "They were willing to take great risks to discover what others had never seen."

B "On some tours, visitors had to crawl on their hands and knees through a passage for more than twenty feet."

C "When they looked up at the ceiling, it seemed that stars were glittering in a night sky."

D "The next generations of Bransfords, as well as many other African Americans, gave tours until the 1930s when the U.S. National Park Service took over."

7 Why did the author **most likely** organize the text with headings?

A to help readers follow the phases of Mammoth Cave's history

B to show differences between Franklin Gorin and John Croghan

C to focus on the role of the National Park Service

D to highlight the different natural features of the cave

GO ON →

8   The following question has two parts. First, answer part A. Then, answer part B.

Part A: Read the sentence from the text.

The young men showed visitors the strange <u>subterranean</u> fish and shrimp living in the cave's waters.

The Latin root *terra* means "earth." What is the meaning of the word <u>subterranean</u>?

A   able to see in the dark

B   unique to the cave

C   underground

D   difficult to see

Part B: Which sentences from the text **best** support your answer in part A? Select **two** options.

A   "They named passageways, such as Grand Avenue, and rock formations, such as a giant stone column called the Devil's Armchair."

B   "By exploring and talking with visitors who knew about caves, they became familiar with the geology of the cave."

C   "They knew how the cave was formed, and they learned the different types of rocks."

D   "Other tours included a boat ride down an underground river."

E   "The guides delighted in giving visitors a chance to 'try the dark,' which meant leaving the visitors for a few minutes in the pitch black of the caverns."

F   "The guides sometimes sold these fish to tourists to earn money."

GO ON →

9   Complete the cause-and-effect chain using the sentences from the box below.

<table>
<tr><td>Cause:</td></tr>
</table>

↓

<table>
<tr><td>Effect/Cause:</td></tr>
</table>

↓

<table>
<tr><td>Effect/Cause:</td></tr>
</table>

↓

<table>
<tr><td>Effect:</td></tr>
</table>

Sentences:

Many of the cave's passageways, rooms, and rock formations were discovered and named.

The three young men could give knowledgeable tours of the cave.

The explorers became familiar with the cave's geology and animal life.

Stephen Bishop, Mat Bransford, and Nick Bransford explored Mammoth Cave.

GO ON →

10 According to the chart, which tour of Mammoth Cave is most difficult, and which is easiest? Use details from the chart to support your answer.

GO ON →

Read the text. Then answer the questions.

Giving Kids Garden Plots

Jonesville has three community gardens. They bring beauty, fresh produce, and clean air to our town. Currently, only Jonesville residents who are eighteen or older are allowed to apply for a community garden plot. I believe the age minimum should be lowered to twelve so that the young people of our town can contribute fully to this valuable resource.

As the parent of an eleven-year-old who has tended her own plot for three years, I can personally speak to the benefits of giving kids access to gardening space. How will this change affect Jonesville? First, when kids take ownership of something in a developmentally appropriate way, they become eager learners. If we extend garden plot access to young people, our local nurseries and libraries will be busy with teens who seek information about agriculture. Kids thrive when they get to be in charge.

Second, greater access to garden plots will increase residents' engagement in our community. Because kids need support from the adults in their families, each young person will bring the involvement of multiple community members to their plots. As a result, whole families will begin to care about issues that impact our town: water use, waste disposal, public health, and more. Communities thrive when their members are engaged and involved.

I will close with a vision. Picture a fourteen-year-old girl, an eight-year-old boy, and their father. They head to the nursery for some vegetable seeds. They go to the community garden, where the girl knows the ropes. She supervises the planting of the seeds. Throughout the growing season, the girl and her family tend the seedlings and mature plants. While harvesting the vegetables, they cook healthy meals and share produce with their friends. The girl and boy learn how to recycle food matter and yard waste by making compost. They then use this compost as a natural fertilizer for their garden plot.

GO ON →

Jonesville City Council, the ball is in your court. Please consider all the benefits of a community garden that truly includes all members of the community. You can make this happen!

GO ON →

11 The following question has two parts. First, answer part A. Then, answer part B.

Part A: Which statement **best** describes the author's point of view about education?

A Giving kids too much work and responsibility at an early age could cause them to lose interest in a subject.

B Giving kids hands-on experience and responsibilities will make them excited to learn more.

C Kids will be more eager to learn if they are able to explore a subject without the direction of an adult.

D Kids will earn higher grades in school if they are allowed access to a community garden.

Part B: Which sentence from the text **best** supports your answer in part A?

A "As the parent of an eleven-year-old who has tended her own plot for three years, I can personally speak to the benefits of giving kids access to gardening space."

B "First, when kids take ownership of something in a developmentally appropriate way, they become eager learners."

C "Second, greater access to garden plots will increase residents' engagement in our community."

D "Because kids need support from the adults in their families, each young person will bring the involvement of multiple community members to their plots."

GO ON →

12 The following question has two parts. First, answer part A. Then, answer part B.

Part A: Read the sentence from the text.

If we extend garden plot access to young people, our local nurseries and libraries will be busy with teens who seek information about <u>agriculture</u>.

The Latin root *agr* means "field." What is the meaning of the word <u>agriculture</u>?

A   the practice of eating only plant products

B   the practice of managing nature preserves

C   the practice of using land to grow food

D   the practice of learning about a topic

Part B: Which sentence from the text **best** helps you understand the meaning of <u>agriculture</u>?

A   "Kids thrive when they get to be in charge."

B   "As a result, whole families will begin to care about issues that impact our town: water use, waste disposal, public health, and more."

C   "Communities thrive when their members are engaged and involved."

D   "While harvesting the vegetables, they cook healthy meals and share produce with their friends."

GO ON →

13 Read the paragraph from the text.

Second, greater access to garden plots will increase residents' engagement in our community. Because kids need support from the adults in their families, each young person will bring the involvement of multiple community members to their plots. As a result, whole families will begin to care about issues that impact our town: water use, waste disposal, public health, and more. Communities thrive when their members are engaged and involved.

What does the cause-and-effect text structure of this paragraph help illustrate about kids' involvement in community gardens?

A Their involvement will lead to more people who care about the issues that face the community.

B Their involvement will increase the popularity of the community and help the town grow.

C Their involvement will produce more varieties of healthy food for the community to eat.

D Their involvement will create more compost and waste that will take more effort to remove.

GO ON →

14   Read the excerpt from the text. Underline **two** context clues that help the reader understand the meanings of the idioms "knows the ropes" and "the ball is in your court."

I will close with a vision. Picture a fourteen-year-old girl, an eight-year-old boy, and their father. They head to the nursery for some vegetable seeds. They go to the community garden, where the girl knows the ropes. She supervises the planting of the seeds. Throughout the growing season, the girl and her family tend the seedlings and mature plants. While harvesting the vegetables, they cook healthy meals and share produce with their friends. The girl and boy learn how to recycle food matter and yard waste by making compost. They then use this compost as a natural fertilizer for their garden plot.

Jonesville City Council, the ball is in your court. Please consider all the benefits of a community garden that truly includes all members of the community. You can make this happen!

15   How does the diagram support the author's purpose?

   A   by highlighting the connection between community gardens and public health

   B   by educating readers about different types of seeds to plant

   C   by showing how the current Jonesville community gardens are organized

   D   by illustrating the author's vision of kids showing ownership of a garden plot

GO ON →

The text below needs revision. Read the text. Then answer the questions.

(1) Have you ever wanted to know more about your ethnic background? (2) Are you interested in taking a test to find out your likelihood of getting a certain disease? (3) If you answered yes to either question you might consider investing in a DNA test kit. (4) Just twenty years ago, kits like this weren't available.

(5) Today they are one of the most handiest tools for learning more about our bodies and backgrounds.

(6) DNA is short for deoxyribonucleic acid. (7) DNA contains the genetic material of a living being. (8) DNA holds the key to all of the traits you inherit from parents, grandparents, and other ancestors. (9) If you want to know about your genes, talking to family members is a good way to find out—but taking a genetic test is a much gooder way.

(10) Here is how a DNA test kit works: First, you order it online. (11) Second, you mail a sample of your saliva to the company that makes the kit. (12) Third, the company tests your DNA. (13) Finally, you receive a personalized report on your ancestry and/or health.

(14) DNA testing kits are becoming extremely popular. (15) In 2008, *time* magazine included a DNA testing kit in its list of the year's best inventions. (16) In 2017, just one DNA testing company sold 1.5 million kits between Black Friday (the day after Thanksgiving) and Cyber Monday (the Monday after Thanksgiving). (17) Most test kits cost between $100 and $200.

GO ON →

Student Name ____

16   What is the correct way to write sentence 3?

  A   If you answered yes of either question you might consider investing in a DNA test kit.

  B   If you answered yes to either question, you might consider investing in a DNA test kit.

  C   If you answered yes to either question you might consider investing in a dna test kit.

  D   If you answered yes to either question you might consider investing, in a DNA test kit.

17   What is the **best** way to write sentence 5?

  A   Today they are one of the handiest tools for learning more about our bodies and backgrounds.

  B   Today they are one of the most handier tools for learning more about our bodies and backgrounds.

  C   Today they are one of the handy tools for learning more about our bodies and backgrounds.

  D   Today they are one of the more handier tools for learning more about our bodies and backgrounds.

18   What is the **best** way to combine sentences 6 and 7 using an appositive?

  A   DNA is short for deoxyribonucleic acid, and DNA contains the genetic material of a living being.

  B   DNA is short for deoxyribonucleic acid; it contains the genetic material of a living being.

  C   DNA, deoxyribonucleic acid, and genetic material of a living being.

  D   DNA, or deoxyribonucleic acid, contains the genetic material of a living being.

GO ON →

19   What is the **best** way to write sentence 9?

  A   If you want to know about your genes; talking to family members is a good way to find out—but taking a genetic test is a much gooder way.

  B   If you want to know about your genes, talking to family members is a good way to find out but taking a genetic test is a much gooder way.

  C   If you want to know about your genes, talking to family members is a good way to find out—but taking a genetic test is a much better way.

  D   If you want to know about your genes, talking to family members is a good way to find out—but taking a genetic test is a more good way.

20   What is the correct way to write sentence 15?

  A   In 2008 *time* magazine included a dna testing kit in its list of the year's best inventions.

  B   In 2008, *time* magazine included a DNA testing kit in it's list of the year's best inventions.

  C   In 2008, *time* magazine included a DNA testing kit in its list of the years' best inventions.

  D   In 2008, *Time* magazine included a DNA testing kit in its list of the year's best inventions.

Informational Performance Task

Task:

Your science class has been learning about how one small change in an environment can disrupt the balance of nature. Your teacher has asked everyone in the class to look up information about plants and animals introduced, purposely or by accident, to the United States, and their effect on the environment.

For this task, you will be writing an informational article related to the topic of invasive plants and animals. Before you write your article, you will review three sources that provide information about the topic.

After you have reviewed these sources, you will answer some questions about them. Briefly scan the sources and the three questions that follow. Then, go back and read the sources carefully to gain the information you will need to answer the questions and write an article.

In Part 2, you will write an informational article on a topic related to the sources.

Directions for Part 1

You will now read several sources. You can re-examine any of the sources as often as you like.

Research Questions:

After examining the sources, use the remaining time in Part 1 to answer three questions about them. Your answers to these questions will be scored. Also, your answers will help you think about the research sources you have read, which should help you write your informational article.

You may refer to the sources when you think it would be helpful. You may also refer to your notes.

GO ON →

Source #1: The New King of the River

In the 1970s, some Southern catfish farmers brought a newcomer, the Asian carp, to the United States. The farmers intended to use the carp to eat unwanted plants crowding their ponds. At first, their plan worked well. The carp feasted on the tiny, microscopic plants called algae and controlled their growth.

However, in time, a period of flooding occurred in the South, and the farmers' private ponds overflowed. Unfortunately, Asian carp escaped into nearby steams. Before long, they made their way into the Mississippi River.

An Ideal Environment

The Mississippi River offered the carp a perfect home. The greedy fish found ample food and devoured algae as well as other aquatic plants. In addition, the friendly, slow-moving river did not contain any threatening predators; no fish in North America was large enough to eat an adult carp.

Unchecked, the carp population thrived. A large female carp is capable of producing a million eggs each year, so their numbers exploded. The carp spread, traveling up the Mississippi River and into connecting waterways.

A Destructive Force

Today, the imported fish has continued to flourish, but its habits are destroying the balance of nature in different rivers. The carp digest their food very rapidly, so food passes quickly through their system. As a result, the fish constantly feeds and can consume up to forty percent of its body weight in a day.

Other small fish living in the rivers depend on the same plants for their food source, but they cannot compete with the ravenous carp. Without enough food to eat, the population of small fish has dropped. In turn, animals like turtles and birds, which eat small fish, also have less food.

The carp's continuous feeding strips away plants growing near shorelines, too. These plants are a key part of the habitat. They slow the movement of the stream. Without them, the rushing water begins to wash away riverbanks.

GO ON →

Problems for People

Asian carp also cause some unusual problems for people. One type of Asian carp is nicknamed the "flying fish." Loud noises, such as rumbling boat engines, startle the fish, which often swim together. When they are frightened, dozens of them suddenly soar into the air, jumping as high as ten feet. While such displays sound entertaining, the heavy, large fish have leapt into unsuspecting boats and struck their passengers, causing injuries.

A Dangerous Possibility

Over time, the Asian Carp has become the dominant fish in various rivers. For instance, ninety percent of the fish in the Illinois River are carp. Currently, a canal connects the Illinois River to Lake Michigan. People are very concerned the carp will enter Lake Michigan through the canal and slowly travel to other, adjoining Great Lakes.

Taking Steps

To prevent the problem, scientists have installed some steel bands that stretch across the canal entry. They produce an electric current that drives the carp back. At the same time, ships can still travel through the useful canal.

However, many people believe the canal should have a solid barrier. The Army Corps of Engineers has proposed building a series of fences. It would take 25 years to construct them. Other attempted control measures include netting carp and encouraging fishing.

Regrettably, the Asian carp is now a permanent resident in North America. Hopefully, with careful measures, people can limit its range. The future of a healthy Great Lakes habitat depends on it.

GO ON →

Source #2: A Super Bird

People know exactly how European starlings arrived in North America. One man, Eugene Schieffelin, is responsible for introducing the bird. The businessman had a peculiar scheme; he wanted to bring all the birds described in William Shakespeare's writings to our country. Some of the birds he imported, such as skylarks, disappeared and died.

However, the immigrant starling fared well. In 1891, Schieffelin released eighty of these birds in Central Park in New York City. A year later, excited birdwatchers discovered the first nesting pair of starlings across the street from the park in the eaves of a museum. In the years to come, the starlings spread much farther than people ever imagined possible. They reached the west coast of California, traveled north to Alaska, and journeyed south to Florida.

Built for Success

How did the starling manage to swiftly adapt and prosper? The bird's physical characteristics provide it with certain advantages. First, the sturdy starling has more muscle than other similar-sized birds. As a result, it easily chases native birds from their prized homes, often stealing nests from bluebirds and woodpeckers.

The starling also has a sharp, strong bill. It can close its beak with enough force to crush its food. In addition, the starling can open its beak with surprising power. Using this trick, the starling creates gashes in the earth and aptly digs for insects, seeds, and other hidden fare.

Finally, the starling has excellent eyesight. Its eyes angle forward more than other birds' eyes do, giving the starling better frontal vision. The starling's eyes also have an unusual ability. One part of its eye can clearly see nearby objects, while another part of the eye is focusing on distant things. Because of this, starlings can effectively hunt for food and watch for danger at the same time.

Flocks of Problems

The starling's abilities have made it very successful at surviving. Often, the hearty birds raise two or three families a year. In the spring and fall, the social birds gather in large flocks, which may number in the thousands.

GO ON →

The vast groups of starlings cause a range of serious problems. At times, starlings descend on farmers' fields; the birds devour growing wheat and steal grain from cattle's troughs. They gobble orchards of cherries, vineyards of grapes, and tons of potatoes. Each year, starlings eat crops that are worth about 800 million dollars.

On occasion, enormous flocks of starlings take over town parks or choose roosting areas near homes or on city buildings. Their droppings soil the walkways and areas below them. Besides being dirty, the droppings carry diseases and present health hazards.

A Losing Battle

Chasing off flocks of starlings is extremely difficult. Many different methods have failed, such as frightening them with balloons, broadcasting threatening sounds, or spraying them with water. In the past, people have even tried putting electric wires or itching powder on buildings to discourage the nuisance birds from roosting. Sometimes, trained wildlife workers must trap and remove the unwanted birds.

Today, scientists estimate that 200 million starlings live in North America. Unfortunately, Schieffelin's eighty original birds are now one of the most abundant species in our country.

GO ON →

Source #3: Invasive Plants and Animals

The following information is part of a presentation on preventing the spread of invasive plants and animals.

Invasive Plants and Animals

How People Can Prevent and Help Stop Their Spread

Invasive Plants and Animals

They are plants and animals that are not native to the environment.

They damage habitats by:

- replacing native animals and plants
- upsetting food webs
- decreasing the water quality of streams and lakes
- introducing new diseases

A common plant invader called Kudzu

GO ON →

How do invasive plants and animals arrive in North America?

Foreign plants and animals enter our country many ways.

- Some were brought to control animal or plant pests.

- Some were brought as pets.

- Some were accidently brought on ships.

- Some were accidently brought on imported plants and goods.

Once these invaders take hold, they are difficult to eliminate. Their numbers can explode. Today, about 4,300 invasive species live in North America.

Taking Important Steps

People can play a key role in limiting this serious problem.

- Do not release imported or exotic pets into the wild or take pets into protected wildlife areas.

- Never transport firewood from one region to another. The wood can be home to unwanted insects.

- In gardens, avoid growing non-native plants that produce lots of seeds that can spread to other areas.

- Do not bring home plants or animals from your vacation site when you travel.

- Volunteer with local park services and help remove invading plants in parks and recreational areas.

GO ON →

1 Draw a line between each Source #1 main idea and the detail from Source #3 that supports it.

Source #1 Main Idea **Source #3 Detail**

Once introduced to an environment, non-native wildlife can rapidly reproduce.

"Once these invaders take hold, they are difficult to eliminate."

Removing non-native wildlife can be a challenging task.

"People can play a key role in limiting this serious problem."

Citizens must work together to prevent the spread of non-native plants.

"Their numbers can explode."

2 Source #1 and Source #2 both describe new ideas that were meant to create a positive change. Explain how each idea created a change in an unexpected way.

____

____

____

____

____

____

GO ON →

3   Explain why it is important to stop the spread of invasive plants and animals. Use at least **one** example from each source to support your explanation. For **each** example, include the source title or number.

____

____

____

____

____

____

GO ON →

Directions for Part 2

You will now review your notes and sources, and plan, draft, revise, and edit your article. You may use your notes and refer to the sources as often as you need.

Now read your assignment and the information about how your informational article will be scored; then begin your work.

Your Assignment:

Your class is studying invasive plants and animals. Your teacher has asked you to write a multi-paragraph article explaining how bringing foreign plants or animals into an environment may affect all living things. The audience for your article will be your classmates and your teacher. In your article, clearly state your main idea and support your main idea with details using information from what you have read.

Now you are going to write your article to submit to your teacher. Choose the most important information from all three sources to support your ideas. Then, write an informational article that is several paragraphs long. Clearly organize your article and support your ideas with details from the sources. Use your own words except when quoting directly from the sources. Be sure to give the source title or number when including details from the sources.

REMEMBER: A well-written informational article

- has a clear main idea
- is well-organized and stays on the topic
- has an introduction and a conclusion
- uses transitions
- uses details from the sources to support your main idea
- develops ideas clearly
- uses clear language
- follows rules of writing (spelling, punctuation, and grammar)

Now begin work on your informational article. Manage your time carefully so that you can plan, write, revise, and edit the final draft of your informational article. Write your response on a separate sheet of paper.

Read the text. Then answer the questions.

Amelia Earhart and the Huckleberry Milkshake

My name is Charlie McNamara, and I'm the luckiest eleven-year-old boy on this magnificent planet, in this magnificent year of 1934. You've probably started to wonder why I claim to be so incredibly lucky, so I'll tell you: I believe myself to be the only person who's ever shared a huckleberry milkshake with Ms. Amelia Earhart.

It's unbelievable that this happened to me, given my humble station in life. I'm just a junior ranch hand here at the Double D guest ranch near Meeteetse, Wyoming. But I've got witnesses to prove that I did indeed split a shake with our nation's famous pilot.

It happened like this: one afternoon about three weeks ago, I went around back of the Double D owner's house for a little shut-eye, and I was amazed to find the most luxurious automobile I'd ever seen roll up the owner's driveway. Out of that automobile stepped a woman wearing boots, pants, a leather jacket, a scarf, and a short haircut.

Could it be?! My mind zipped back to the moment I'd first heard about this very woman.

It's May 1932. Waving a newspaper in his hand, Jody comes zooming into the barn. "Did you see this, boys?" he marvels breathlessly, pointing to a photograph on the front page. "A woman named Amelia Earhart just flew by herself across the Atlantic Ocean! She's only the second person to cross the Atlantic solo in an airplane!"

We approach Jody slowly—it's a cowpoke's job to appear unimpressed—and take a gander at the photograph. It's Ms. Earhart, looking chipper and confident, standing on her Lockheed 5B Vega in Ireland, where she'd landed after a 15-hour flight. I just know she and her plane are laughing, thinking, "You thought we couldn't do it, world? Well, the joke's on you!"

And two years later, not 100 feet away from me, here was that same woman. That aviator jacket, that hair, those sparkling eyes, that adventurous expression . . . it was undeniably Ms. Amelia Earhart!

"Welcome to the Double D, ma'am, and sir," I heard the ranch owner say. "We're honored you've chosen to stay with us—"

That was all I needed to hear. I ran to tell all the boys, who forgot to act unimpressed, and then I did what any ranch hand would do if the most famous woman in the world was staying at his ranch: I high-tailed it to the general store to buy a new shirt. It cost me four weeks of wages, but I didn't care; I even bought myself a huckleberry milkshake to sweeten the moment.

GO ON →

I rushed back, and just as I opened the front gate, who did I see touring the ranch but Ms. Earhart, her husband, and the owner. Star-struck, I froze in place; my jaw dropped so low I had to push it back up with my hand.

That's when Ms. Earhart walked right up to me, shook my hand, and said, "My name is Amelia. I've heard this town's got some fantastic huckleberry milkshakes. Would you happen to be drinking one of them right now?"

"Why, y-y-yes, ma'am," I stammered.

"May I trouble you to give it a try?" asked America's hero.

"C-c-certainly, ma'am," I heard myself say, handing over the cup of purple frosty goodness with the same hand that shook hers a moment earlier.

Ms. Earhart took a long sip and let out a contented sigh. "Whoever told me about these shakes had their reputation right," she affirmed. "Thank you for sharing some with me."

I barely saw Ms. Earhart during the rest of her stay at the Double D. But, I tell you the truth, I could do no wrong among all the cowpokes after that day. For weeks I felt like I was flying in one of Ms. Earhart's planes—I still do today. And I still chuckle to know that my encounter with a hero never would have happened if I hadn't gone out for that silly huckleberry milkshake.

Amelia Earhart, 1936

GO ON →

1   The following question has two parts. First, answer part A. Then, answer part B.

Part A: Read the paragraph from the text.

It's unbelievable that this happened to me, given my <u>humble</u> station in life. I'm just a junior ranch hand here at the Double D guest ranch near Meeteetse, Wyoming. But I've got witnesses to prove that I did indeed split a shake with our nation's famous pilot.

What is the meaning of the word <u>humble</u> in this paragraph?

A   lowly

B   unlucky

C   difficult

D   unique

Part B: Which phrase from the paragraph **best** hints at the meaning of <u>humble</u>?

A   "unbelievable that this happened"

B   "just a junior ranch hand"

C   "witnesses to prove"

D   "split a shake"

GO ON →

2   The following question has two parts. First, answer part A. Then, answer part B.

Part A: What is one important effect of the first-person narration of the text?

A   It suggests that Amelia Earhart was especially popular in small towns like Meeteetse.

B   It gives the story an energetic and star-struck feel due to the narrator's youth.

C   It helps emphasize the sequential order of the plot events.

D   It provides access to the thoughts of multiple characters.

Part B: Which sentence from the text **best** supports your answer in part A?

A   "It cost me four weeks of wages, but I didn't care; I even bought myself a huckleberry milkshake to sweeten the moment."

B   "Ms. Earhart took a long sip and let out a contented sigh."

C   "'Welcome to the Double D, ma'am, and sir,' I heard the ranch owner say."

D   "I barely saw Ms. Earhart during the rest of her stay at the Double D."

GO ON →

3 Read the sentences from the text.

I just know she and her plane are laughing, thinking, "You thought we couldn't do it, world? Well, the joke's on you!"

Why does the author **most likely** use personification in these sentences?

A to give readers a glimpse into Earhart's mind

B to make a comparison between Charlie and Earhart

C to foreshadow later events

D to show Charlie's imagination

4 Mark the boxes to show whether each piece of information is revealed to the reader during the regular action of the text or during Charlie's flashback.

	Revealed During Regular Action	Revealed During Flashback
Amelia Earhart crosses the Atlantic Ocean in an airplane.	☐	☐
Charlie shares a milkshake.	☐	☐
The ranch owner leads tours of the Double D.	☐	☐

5 Which statement **best** expresses a main theme of the text?

A One should avoid showing too much emotion in public.

B Young people tend to exaggerate about things.

C Chance encounters can change a person's life.

D Pride gets in the way of enjoying moments fully.

GO ON →

Read the text. Then answer the questions.

Breaking Barriers

Elizabeth Blackwell listened to her friend's unusual advice. He said that she should disguise herself as a man if she wanted to study and become a doctor! It was 1845, and only men attended medical school. However, Blackwell absolutely refused to participate in the dishonest scheme. She wanted the world to know that a woman could be a capable doctor, too.

Childhood Lessons

Blackwell was born in England in 1821. At that time, few women focused on school studies. Fortunately, Blackwell's father believed that women should have a wide education. He hired tutors to teach all his children challenging subjects like mathematics and Latin. Blackwell loved learning, and she developed a passion for reading.

When Blackwell was eleven years old, her family moved to America. She continued her education, attending an excellent school. When she was just sixteen, she became a teacher. It was one of the few acceptable careers for a woman. Blackwell was skilled at her job, but she felt restless. One day, a sick woman inspired Blackwell to pursue a new goal. She suggested that Blackwell use her sharp mind to become a doctor.

Battling for a Chance

Blackwell's close friends gently told her that her new dream was impossible for a woman, but Blackwell was not discouraged. She began reading and studying medical textbooks. One doctor, persuaded by her dedication, allowed Blackwell to attend his medical lectures and use his library. At the same time, Blackwell sent in applications to medical schools around the country.

Sadly, Blackwell received sixteen letters of rejection. Finally, the Geneva Medical College in New York accepted her as a student. Blackwell did not know it, but the male students at the school thought her letter was a silly joke. When asked by teachers to vote on the issue, they laughed and shouted, "Yes."

Classroom Struggles

At the college, Blackwell concentrated on her studies. If paper airplanes winged her way, she brushed them aside. When professors told her a woman should not witness certain operations, she wrote letters to convince them otherwise. When people in town ignored the woman with the strange ambition, Blackwell treated them in a polite, quiet manner.

GO ON →

As the weeks passed, Blackwell's fellow students grew to respect and admire their hardworking classmate. Two years later, Blackwell graduated at the top of her class. She became the first woman in the country to obtain a medical degree.

Changing Views

The newspapers wrote favorably about Blackwell's achievement, and the public was impressed. Like a small crack in a dike, Blackwell's success opened the way for others. In the next few years, several more medical schools accepted women students. The views of a woman's abilities were shifting.

Throughout her life, Blackwell continued to be a pioneer in the medical field. She championed the education of women and their care. She also directed attention at preventing disease by teaching others about washing hands. Always, Blackwell faced any challenges with determination. She once wrote that if an idea was valuable, "there must be some way of realizing it!"

GO ON →

6   How does the author support the idea that Blackwell's father influenced her future career as a doctor? Support your answer with details from the text.

____

____

____

____

____

7   The following question has two parts. First, answer part A. Then, answer part B.

Part A: Read the sentence from the text.

One day, a sick woman inspired Blackwell to <u>pursue</u> a new goal.

What does the word <u>pursue</u> mean in the sentence?

A   follow close behind

B   create a change

C   learn all about

D   try to achieve

Part B: Which sentence from the text **best** helps you understand the meaning of <u>pursue</u>?

A   "It was one of the few acceptable careers for a woman."

B   "She began reading and studying medical textbooks."

C   "Blackwell did not know it, but the male students at the school thought her letter was a silly joke."

D   "Like a small crack in a dike, Blackwell's success opened the way for others."

GO ON →

8 Read the sentences from the text. Circle the word that is a homophone of a word that means "in a voice that can be heard" or "loudly."

One doctor, persuaded by her dedication, allowed Blackwell to attend his medical lectures and use his library. At the same time, Blackwell sent in applications to medical schools around the country.

9 The following question has two parts. First, answer part A. Then, answer part B.

Part A: How did Blackwell respond to the obstacles she faced at the medical college?

A She kept trying even when people opposed her.

B She became friendly with her classmates.

C She studied longer than her classmates in order to graduate.

D She tried to prove she was the smartest student in the class.

Part B: Which sentence from the text **best** supports your answer in part A?

A "At the college, Blackwell concentrated on her studies."

B "When professors told her a woman should not witness certain operations, she wrote letters to convince them otherwise."

C "As the weeks passed, Blackwell's fellow students grew to respect and admire their hardworking classmate."

D "Two years later, Blackwell graduated at the top of her class."

GO ON →

10   The following question has two parts. First, answer part A. Then, answer part B.

Part A: Why does the author describe the attitudes of the public?

    A   to show that Blackwell faced more struggles than most people did

    B   to describe how Blackwell's achievements made her famous

    C   to explain how Blackwell proved to people that women were fine teachers

    D   to demonstrate that Blackwell helped people accept the idea of women doctors

Part B: Which sentence from the text **best** supports your answer in part A?

    A   "The newspapers wrote favorably about Blackwell's achievement, and the public was impressed."

    B   "In the next few years, several more medical schools accepted women students."

    C   "She also directed attention at preventing disease by teaching others about washing hands."

    D   "Always, Blackwell faced any challenges with determination."

GO ON →

Read the text. Then answer the questions.

from "Vacation Time"
by Edgar Guest

Vacation time! How glad it seemed
When as a boy I sat and dreamed
Above my school books, of the fun
That I should claim when toil was done;

5   And, Oh, how oft my youthful eye
Went wandering with the patch of sky
That drifted by the window panes
O'er pleasant fields and dusty lanes,
Where I would race and romp and shout

10   The very moment school was out.
My artful little fingers then
Feigned[1] labor with the ink and pen,
But heart and mind were far away,
Engaged in some glad bit of play.

15   The last two weeks dragged slowly by;
Time hadn't then learned how to fly.
It seemed the clock upon the wall
From hour to hour could only crawl,
And when the teacher called my name,

20   Unto my cheeks the crimson came,
For I could give no answer clear
To questions that I didn't hear.
"Wool gathering, were you?" oft she said
And smiled to see me blushing red.

25   Her voice had roused me from a dream
Where I was fishing in a stream,
And, if I now recall it right,
Just at the time I had a bite.

---

[1] faked

"Vacation Time" from *Just Folks* by Edgar A. Guest. Reilly & Lee Co., Chicago, 1917.

GO ON →

11   The following question has two parts. First, answer part A. Then, answer part B.

Part A: Read the lines from the poem.

Unto my cheeks the <u>crimson</u> came,
For I could give no answer clear
To questions that I didn't hear.

What is the meaning of the word <u>crimson</u>?

A   nervousness

B   thought

C   fever

D   purplish-red

Part B: Which word from the poem **best** supports your answer in part A?

A   "mind"

B   "Wool"

C   "blushing"

D   "dream"

GO ON →

12 Complete the chart to show which lines contain personification. Mark the boxes to show what is being personified in each line. Not all lines contain personification.

	fields	lanes	heart	mind	clock	wall
"O'er pleasant fields and dusty lanes, / Where I would race and romp and shout"	☐	☐	☐	☐	☐	☐
"But heart and mind were far away, / Engaged in some glad bit of play."	☐	☐	☐	☐	☐	☐
"It seemed the clock upon the wall / From hour to hour could only crawl,"	☐	☐	☐	☐	☐	☐

13 What is hidden from the reader as a result of the poem being told from a first-person point of view? Select **two** options.

A the other students' feelings

B the appearance of the clock

C the teacher's reaction to the speaker

D the details of the speaker's dream

E the teacher's opinion of the speaker

F the amount of time left in the school year

GO ON →

14   What is one important effect of the rhyme scheme of the poem?

   A   It emphasizes the frustrating length of the school year.

   B   It helps the reader visualize details about the speaker's school.

   C   It creates a song-like feel that adds to the speaker's excitement.

   D   It focuses the reader on the most important words in the poem.

15   The following question has two parts. First, answer part A. Then, answer part B.

Part A: What is a theme in the poem?

   A   Familiar surroundings bring comfort.

   B   Learning new things can be exciting.

   C   Growing up can be painful.

   D   Anticipation can lead to daydreams.

Part B: Which excerpt from the poem **best** supports your answer in part A?

   A   "When as a boy I sat and dreamed
Above my school books, of the fun
That I should claim when toil was done;"

   B   "The last two weeks dragged slowly by;
Time hadn't then learned how to fly."

   C   "And when the teacher called my name,
Unto my cheeks the crimson came,
For I could give no answer clear"

   D   "'Wool gathering, were you?' oft she said
And smiled to see me blushing red."

GO ON →

The text below needs revision. Read the text. Then answer the questions.

(1) As the first rays of sun peeked over the mountain, Isidora ran across the pueblo to the home of her friend Carmen. (2) Today was the day: Isidora was going to make pottery!

(3) Carmen's mother Josefa was known for her pottery. (4) At every feast day, people admired Josefa's bowls most than anyone else's. (5) Isidora and Carmen had begged Josefa for years to teach them.

(6) Isidora burst into Josefa's kitchen and found Carmen standing next to a bench with tools on it. (7) Josefa was standing there too. (8) Everything appeared to be ready!

(9) "All right, girls," Josefa announced, "we're going to start with bowls. (10) In a month, you can choose your favorite bowl for the feast day. (11) Therefore, first I must warn you that making pottery is harder than it looks. (12) Don't be surprised if your first bowl isn't perfect."

(13) Josefa showed the girls how to find the best clay, and they dug enough clay to make three bowls. (14) They were proud to dig Josefa's clay for she.

(15) Back in Josefa's kitchen, the hardest part began: shaping the clay. (16) When Isidora eventually got the curve correct, part of her bowl collapsed.

(17) "But I didn't do nothing wrong!" Isidora exclaimed.

(18) "This is only the first day," Josefa comforted Isidora. (19) "Come back tomorrow, and I promise, you will get better."

GO ON →

16   What is the correct way to write sentence 4?

   A   At every feast day, people admired Josefas' bowls most than
anyone else's.

   B   At every feast day, people admired Josefa's bowls more than
anyone else's.

   C   At every feast day, people admired Josefa's bowls more than
anyone elses.

   D   At every feast day, people admired Josefa's bowls most than
anyone elses.

17   What is the **best** way to combine sentences 6 and 7?

   A   Isidora burst into Josefa's kitchen and found Carmen standing next to a
bench with tools on it, and Josefa was standing there too.

   B   Josefa was standing there when Isidora burst into Josefa's kitchen and
found Carmen standing next to a bench with tools on it.

   C   Isidora burst into Josefa's kitchen, and Isidora found Carmen standing
next to a bench with tools on it, and Josefa was standing there too.

   D   Isidora burst into Josefa's kitchen and found Carmen and Josefa standing
next to a bench with tools on it.

18   What is the **best** way to write sentence 11?

   A   Similarly, first I must warn you that making pottery is harder than
it looks.

   B   Otherwise, first I must warn you that making pottery is harder than
it looks.

   C   However, first I must warn you that making pottery is harder than it looks.

   D   Still, first I must warn you that making pottery is harder than it looks.

GO ON →

19   What is the correct way to write sentence 14?

   A   They were proud to dig Josefa's clay for them.

   B   They are proud to dig Josefa's clay for she.

   C   They were proud to dig Josefa's clay for her.

   D   They were proud to dig Josefa's clay for they.

20   What is the **best** way to write sentence 17?

   A   "But I did'nt do nothing wrong!" Isidora exclaimed.

   B   "But I didn't do anything wrong!" Isidora exclaimed.

   C   "But I didn't do nothing wrong?" Isidora exclaimed.

   D   "But I didn't do everything wrong!" Isidora exclaimed.

Opinion Performance Task

Task:

Your class has been learning about ways people affect the environment. Now the mayor has proposed a plan to build a new highway near your town. As editor of the school newspaper, you have decided to write a multi-paragraph article to give an opinion about the mayor's proposal. Before you begin, you do some research and find two articles and a presentation about how the changes humans make can affect animals and plants living around them.

After you have reviewed these sources, you will answer some questions about them. Briefly scan the sources and the three questions that follow. Then, go back and review the sources carefully to gain the information you will need to answer the questions and finalize your research. You may take notes on the information you find in the sources as you read. Your notes will be available to you as you answer the questions.

Directions for Part 1

You will now examine three sources. You can look at these sources as often as you like.

Research Questions:

After examining the sources, use the rest of the time in Part 1 to answer the three questions. Your answers to these questions will be scored. Also, your answers will help you think about the information you have read and viewed, which should help you write your article.

You may take notes when you think it would be helpful.

GO ON →

Source #1: An Invisible Pollution

Cities throb with sound. Airplanes thunder overhead, traffic rumbles by, and horns blare. As populations grow, these noise levels constantly increase. They are an invisible type of pollution that upsets the balance of nature.

Hearing, a Valuable Sense

Most animals have well-developed hearing. They depend on this sharp sense to avoid danger, and, sometimes, loud sounds interfere with their ability to escape predators.

For example, scientists studied how dune buggy noise affected the desert kangaroo rat. First, they exposed the rat to bursts of the noise. Then they tested how quickly the rat responded to the *swish* of an approaching snake. Usually, the rat kicks sand at this enemy when it is about sixteen inches away. However, after listening to blasts of a dune buggy, the rat did not react until the snake crept within an inch. This is a severe disadvantage for the endangered rat.

For some animals, loud noises prevent their mating success. Certain animals rely on mating calls to attract partners, but noise masks their songs. This is especially true for several species of tree frogs, and scientists say the noise could eventually lead to decreases in frog populations.

Other animals, like the German nightingale, have attempted to overcome city noises by singing with more piercing melodies. Their songs now reach 95 decibels, the same volume as a roaring chainsaw. Certain birds have tried changing the pitch of their songs, too, or singing at night after daytime sounds fade. By adjusting their calls, the birds may be able to survive noisy challenges.

Changing Habits

Loud noises cause animals to modify other behaviors, too. Today, aircraft frequently fly over wildlife regions. Their constant rumbling can upset animals living beneath their flight patterns. As a result, some animals, like the endangered palila bird in Hawaii, leave prime nesting locations and crowd into peaceful, less-suitable areas.

In some cases, low-flying planes frighten herds of animals, causing stampedes. The frantic racing leads to injuries. This is a special concern when planes disrupt herds with young calves. One study tracked several caribou herds. The herd that experienced the most overhead flights lost the most calves.

GO ON →

Links in a Chain

When one animal alters its behavior, the change can ripple through the environment. Scientists unraveled a perfect example when they studied the relationship between hummingbirds, Western scrub jays, mice, and pinyon pine trees. The loud noise from natural gas wells sets off the chain of events.

To begin with, the clatter of the noisy wells chased jays from the surrounding areas; jays preferred quiet settings. Once the jays disappeared, hummingbirds quickly moved into the location. Because jays usually raid their nests, with the jays gone, the noisy sites now favored the hummingbirds. The hummingbirds fed on flowers, spread their pollen, and helped flowers grow.

However, the absence of jays hurt the pine trees. Often, jays eat the trees' seeds and stash extra seeds in the ground, encouraging seedlings to sprout.

After the jay disappeared, mice feasted on the available seeds. Unlike jays, mice left few seeds behind. In time, few seedlings were found near wells. The noisy sound had led to a decrease in the number of pine trees.

How loud is your world?

Today, scientists continue to investigate the impacts of noise pollution. Our government is also working to limit these problems through the Noise Control Act, which has lessened aircraft noise. You can help, too, by turning down the volume of things, like televisions, and by shutting off machines, like fans, when they are not being used.

Look at the decibel measure of some common sounds. Avoid listening to loud noises for long periods when possible.

Sound Source	Degree	Decibel Measure
Aircraft taking off	deafening	180
Thunder	deafening	120
Passing truck	very loud	100
Lawn mower	very loud	100
Average traffic	loud	85
Washing machine	loud	70
Average radio	loud	70
Conversation	moderate	60
Quiet stream	moderate	50

GO ON →

Source #2: Our Dark Night Sky, a Valuable Resource

When you step outside at night, can you see the stars shining in the sky? Or does the orange glow of city lights mask their sparkle? Today, some city skies are thousands of times brighter than 200 years ago. This increasing "light pollution" is a concern because it affects our environment and wildlife.

Life Rhythms

Living things have adapted their habits to fit the daily cycles of light and darkness. For instance, certain animals, like bats, hunt for insects at night when fewer predators will see them. Unfortunately, light pollution can alter these cycles and cause far-reaching effects.

The Quest for Dinner

First, scientists say light pollution can change the timing of an animal's search for food. Some creatures wait until dusk to leave their homes and begin eating. When unexpected lights click on at sunset, the puzzled animals remain hidden and have less time to feed.

Light pollution influences where hungry animals hunt for meals, too. Because animals avoid lights to stay safe, they will pass by convenient meals in bright areas, wandering further to find food. The extra effort burns energy, requiring them to need more food.

Getting Together

Sometimes, light pollution disrupts the mating of animals. The firefly is one likely victim. Around the world, the numbers of this insect have dropped. Fireflies use flashing light patterns to attract mates in the dark. When the night sky is too bright, the blinking signals are difficult to notice, making it more challenging for fireflies to find each other.

Traveling Troubles

Often, light pollution causes problems for animals roaming at night. For instance, deer that encounter traffic cannot see well. Like many nocturnal animals, their eyes magnify light, and bright shining headlights blind them for a moment. Consequently, the deer may accidentally leap in front of a vehicle.

Other animals, like the puma, view the lighted highway like a fence. To survive, pumas require large territories for hunting. However, one scientist noted that when pumas neared lighted highways, they refused to cross. This most likely happened because the brightness hampered the puma's vision. Sadly, brightly lit areas are breaking apart the ranges where numerous animals travel, fragmenting their homes.

GO ON →

Light pollution creates dangerous confusion for traveling, newborn sea turtles, too. When they hatch, the turtles instantly seek the brightest light. In the past, moonlight reflecting on the ocean safely drew them into the water. Today, the gleam from beach homes bewilders the newborn turtles, and they aimlessly wander inland.

Migrating birds flying at night depend on both moonlight and the stars to navigate. However, a city's artificial glow sometimes blocks these guiding lights. Furthermore, shimmering buildings attract birds like magnets. Scientists do not understand why, but birds will circle the glittering building until exhausted. Airport towers and lighthouses present similar hazards.

How Can People Help?

Some big cities have started "Light Out" programs to help birds; building owners voluntarily shut off unnecessary lights during migration seasons. In addition, cities near beaches have passed laws guiding the usage and types of outside lights that people install.

You can reduce the problem by making wise choices in your own home and yard. First, avoid landscape lighting if it is simply decorative. Next, be sure to shut off unneeded lights, or use a timing system. Finally, position lights so their beams shine downward, not into the sky.

Currently 19% of the electricity used in the world is for lights at night. By working together, we may be able to lessen this number and save our dark night sky.

GO ON →

Source #3: Understanding Dams

The following information is part of a presentation on the benefits and drawbacks of dams.

What is considered a dam?

- A dam is a man-made structure that stops the flow of water.

- Once a dam is created, an artificial lake forms behind it.

- In the United States, the National Inventory of Dams (NID) lists 66,000 river dams.

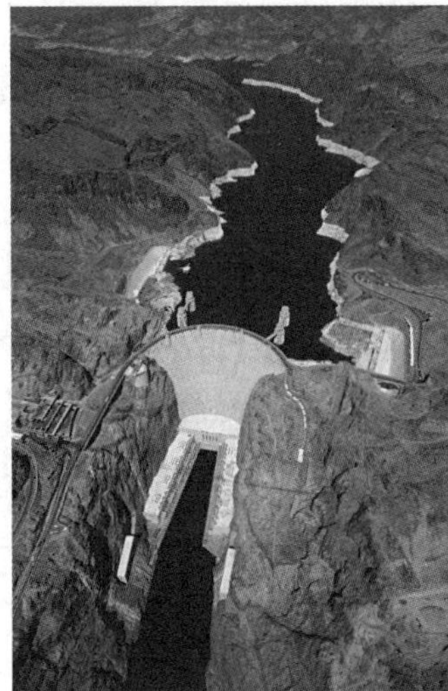

Dams serve multiple purposes

- Dams produce hydroelectricity, a clean, renewable form of energy.
- Dams supply water for crops and household needs.
- Dams allow people to prevent flooding. Dams can control the release of river water.
- Mining operations use dams to catch any pollution they create, so the pollution does not spread into rivers.
- Dams create large lakes for fish.
- Dams provide a new habitat for wildlife.
- Nearly 40% of all dams in our nation are used for recreation.

GO ON →

Dams have drawbacks . . .

- Dams block rivers and limit debris such as twigs, leaves, and mud. Living things depend on debris for food and shelter.

- Dams stop river water from flowing downstream, reducing the depth of the stream. Shallow streams supply less water to the earth, and the groundwater level drops, affecting plants that depend on it.

- A dam's artificial lake floods plants and vegetation once used by wildlife.

- Dams block migrating fish from traveling upstream to lay eggs, and they prevent newly hatched fish from traveling downstream to oceans.

Photo courtesy of USDA Natural Resources Conservation Service

. . . but people are searching for solutions

People are working to solve problems created by dams. Fish "ladders" allow fish to travel around dams. Dams that are no longer useful are removed.

Photo by Gary Wilson, USDA Natural Resources Conservation Service

GO ON →

Unit Assessments

1   Complete the chart to show which sentence from Source #1 and which sentence from Source #2 **best** support this idea.

Pollution can change animal behaviors and their environments.

Best supports the idea	Source #1
☐	"In time, few seedlings were found near wells. "
☐	"Today, scientists continue to investigate the impacts of noise pollution."
☐	"Usually, the rat kicks sand at this enemy when it is about sixteen inches away."
	Source #2
☐	"To survive, pumas require large territories for hunting."
☐	"When they hatch, the turtles instantly seek the brightest light."
☐	"Around the world, the numbers of this insect have dropped."

GO ON →

2 Explain how making changes in our environment can reduce the negative impact on plants and animals living around us. Give **two** examples, one from Source #1 and one from Source #2. For each example, include the source title or number.

____

____

____

____

____

3 In Source #3, the author provides examples of the positive and negative aspects of dams and their effect on the environment. Explain how this provides a different point of view from the other **two** sources. Use details from the text to support your answer.

____

____

____

____

____

GO ON →

Directions for Part 2

You will now review your notes and sources, and plan, draft, revise, and edit your opinion article. You may use your notes and refer to the sources. Now read your assignment and the information about how your writing will be scored; then begin your work.

Your Assignment:

Your town is considering building a new, faster highway system that will save the townspeople time and money. The highway will be built over an existing swamp and includes plans for a new dam. As editor of your school newspaper, you are going to write a multi-paragraph article giving your opinion about this proposal. In your article, you will take a side as to whether you think the idea is a good one or whether it should be reconsidered. The audience for your article will be students, parents, and your community. In your article, clearly state your opinion and support your opinion with reasons that are thoroughly developed using information from what you have read.

Now you are going to write your opinion article. Choose the most important information from all three sources to support your ideas. Then, write an opinion article that is several paragraphs long. Clearly organize your article and support your ideas with details from the sources. Use your own words except when quoting directly from the sources. Be sure to give the source title when using details from the sources.

REMEMBER: A well-written opinion article

- has a clear opinion
- is well-organized and stays on the topic
- has an introduction and conclusion
- uses transitions
- uses details or facts from more than one source to support your opinion
- gives details or facts from the sources in your own words
- gives the title or number of the source for the details or facts you included
- develops ideas clearly
- uses clear language
- follows rules of writing (spelling, punctuation, and grammar usage)

Now begin work on your opinion article. Manage your time carefully so that you can plan, write, revise, and edit the final draft of your article. Write your response on a separate sheet of paper.

Unit 1 Answer Key

Student Name: _______________________________

Question	Correct Answer	Content Focus	Complexity
1	see below	Character, Setting, Plot: Sequence	DOK 1
2	B	Greek and Latin Prefixes	DOK 1
3A	C	Context Clues: Sentence Clues	DOK 2
3B	D	Context Clues: Sentence Clues / Text Evidence	DOK 2
4	B	Character, Setting, Plot: Sequence	DOK 1
5	see below	Literary Elements: Plot	DOK 2
6	see below	Homographs	DOK 1
7	B	Text Structure: Cause and Effect	DOK 2
8A	D	Context Clues: Sentence Clues	DOK 2
8B	A	Context Clues: Sentence Clues / Text Evidence	DOK 2
9A	B	Author's Point of View	DOK 3
9B	E, F	Author's Point of View / Text Evidence	DOK 2
10	C	Text Features: Primary and Secondary Sources	DOK 2
11A	A	Greek and Latin Prefixes	DOK 1
11B	D	Greek and Latin Prefixes / Text Evidence	DOK 1
12	A	Author's Point of View	DOK 3
13	C	Homographs	DOK 1
14A	D	Text Features: Graphs	DOK 2
14B	C	Text Features: Graphs / Text Evidence	DOK 2
15	see below	Text Structure: Cause and Effect	DOK 2
16	C	Correcting Run-on Sentences	DOK 1
17	D	Subjects and Predicates	DOK 1
18	D	Compound Sentences	DOK 1
19	A	Complex Sentences	DOK 1
20	C	Commas	DOK 1

Unit 1 Answer Key   Student Name: _______________________

Comprehension 1, 4, 5, 7, 9A, 9B, 10, 12, 14A, 14B, 15	/18	%
Vocabulary 2, 3A, 3B, 6, 8A, 8B, 11A, 11B, 13	/12	%
English Language Conventions 16, 17, 18, 19, 20	/5	%
Total Unit 1 Assessment Score	/35	%

1 Students should put the story events in the following order:
- 1 - The bobcat hunts the rabbit that Brian's family sees.
- 2 - The family begins hiking with a ranger.
- 3 - The family looks at a rabbit carcass.
- 4 - The family observes a wood stork.
- 5 - Brian concludes that the park has more action than most video games.

5 **2-point response:** Brian's parents smile because, before the camping trip, Brian would have stopped talking to them and responded to the text right away. His parents probably are happy that the camping trip helped Brian develop a little more appreciation for nature and learn that getting away from computers and talking with his family about an interesting subject can be enjoyable and important.

6 Students should complete the chart as follows:
- trip: a journey
- kind: a group of things in the same category

15 Students should complete the chart as follows:
- Cause: Students know they have constant access to tap water at school.—Effect: Students will bring fewer soft drinks and juice to school.
- Cause: Americans are buying more and more bottled water every year.—Effect: Resources such as energy and landfill space are being stretched.
- Cause: Students have no reason to throw away water because they keep their personal bottles with them.—Effect: Students will minimize water waste in their schools.

Unit 1 Answer Key

Student Name: _______________________________

Narrative Performance Task			
Question	**Answer**	**Complexity**	**Score**
1	see below	DOK 2	/1
2	see below	DOK 3	/2
3	see below	DOK 3	/2
Story	see below	DOK 4	/4 [P/O] /4 [D/E] /2 [C]
Total Score			**/15**

1. Students should match the following:
   - Source #1: Federal government was heavily involved in the project
   - Source #2: Wanted little government control or funding
   - Both: Monument is an important part of this nation's history

2. **2-point response:** Source #1 tells how the measurements of the model are used to figure out the size of the statue. For example, "a one-inch eye on the model equaled a 12-foot eye on the mountain." The author also explains how the workers were lowered in chairs into position to do their jobs. "Carefully, ropes lowered the chairs and workers into the correct position on the cliff's face." These details help the reader better understand why a model is a necessary part of the sculpture process. The details about the workers help the reader better understand the dangers of the carving process.

3. **2-point response:** The artists chose certain subjects for their design or positioned them in certain ways to convey their messages. In "The Making of a Monument," Borglum wanted the memorial to tell about America's history, so he carved "presidents who had notably shaped the nation's history," like George Washington, the "Father of the Nation." In "A Story Told in Stone," Ziolkowski wanted his statue to tell the story of the Sioux nation. He carved Crazy Horse so "his finger would point at the lands where his people once lived" to show the lands that were important to the Sioux.

10-point anchor paper: My hands shook with excitement as I stood in my kitchen and read the letter from the mayor. I couldn't wait to start the job. Already, a million ideas raced through my mind. I called immediately to accept the challenge.

"I'm glad you're willing to do this, Abel," the mayor told me. "I have some workers lined up to help you, too, and a studio. Everything is waiting for you at Block Mountain, a small mountain at the edge of town. You should be able to make a spectacular statue on it."

The next morning, I set out for the mountain. As I traveled, I thought about Billy, a young boy who had rescued Mrs. Williams from her burning house. I thought about how brave he must be, and what an amazing accomplishment that was. I also remembered how the famous artist Ziolkowski had decided to carve the statue of Crazy Horse pointing over the Black Hills. The statue showed how the land was special to the Sioux people. The shape of it fit the mountain well. I had to think of a design that would fit into a rectangular block, and my statue had to tell the story of Billy's bravery.

When I arrived at Block Mountain, a man named Davis met me. He was six feet tall, with curly black hair and a beard as a big as a bush.

"I can't wait to start blasting the rock away!" Davis laughed as he grabbed my suitcases and hurried toward the door. He had more energy than an Olympic racer.

Next, we drove to an art studio at the base of the mountain. This was where I could build my model.

"You could carve a statue of just Billy himself," Davis suggested. He recited his ideas in his booming voice until my ears rang. However, I already had my own plan. The next morning, I got to work early in the studio, while it was empty and quiet. I used clay to build my model. I had decided to use a scale where one inch on my model would equal one foot on the mountain. That would make it easy to transfer my design to the mountain.

Quietly, I shaped my clay. After lots of thinking, I had decided to carve a statue of Billy carrying Mrs. Williams to safety, with a burning building in the background.

A week later, I completed my model. Davis had visited me every day and offered his suggestions. Sometimes, I used some of his ideas. For instance, he had told me to make the base of the statue thicker, so the rock would be sturdier. At last, we were ready to start.

First, I gave Davis the key measurements for Billy holding Mrs. Williams. Davis and his workers used ropes and bosun chairs to lower themselves into the right position on the front of the rocky cliff. They used laser beams to measure the points and mark them with bright red paint. After that outline was drawn, they did the same thing for the house. When they finished, I carefully examined them. I studied and decided exactly what stone would have to be blasted away.

The next morning, Davis and his workers started using gel explosives to get rid of the unwanted stone. A bulldozer and truck waited nearby to haul away the rubble and make our job a little easier. Everything was going smoothly until the last blast. A huge lump of stone was left on top of the house.

"We can take care of that tomorrow," Davis said. "That part of the stone had lots of iron in it; we need to use more explosives."

That night, I dreamt about the lump of stone. The next morning, I searched for Davis before he could blast it away. "It's the perfect size for flames," I told him. "I'm going to add it to my design!"

Unit 1 Rationales

1

The following answer is correct because it shows the correct sequential order of events in time: (1) The bobcat hunts the rabbit that Brian's family sees. (The ranger says that bobcats hunt at night, so the bobcat must have hunted the rabbit before the family begins their hike.) (2) The family begins hiking with a ranger. (3) The family looks at a rabbit carcass. (4) The family observes a wood stork. (5) Brian concludes that the park has more action than most video games.

2

A is incorrect because this definition does not make sense in the context of the sentence.

B is correct because "ahead of time" means "before"; the narrator took the precaution of charging his phone before leaving for the trip.

C is incorrect because charging a phone would not be considered "hard work."

D is incorrect because this definition does not make sense in the context of the sentence.

3A

A is incorrect because "hear" is not the meaning of *envision*, and this definition does not make sense given the context clues.

B is incorrect because "feel" is not the meaning of *envision*, and this definition does not make sense given the context clues.

C is correct because "see" is the meaning of *envision* and makes the most sense in the context of the sentence.

D is incorrect because "smell" is not the meaning of *envision*, and this definition does not make sense given the context clues.

3B

A is incorrect because the phrase provides no clue to the meaning of *envision*; *almost* can modify thousands of verbs.

B is incorrect because you can envision just about anything; "fires burning" tells us very little about the meaning of *envision*.

C is incorrect because you can take many different actions while you walk; this phrase tells us almost nothing about the meaning of *envision*.

D is correct because it provides an important clue to the meaning of *envision*: it has to do with seeing something as it happens, like watching a video.

4

A is incorrect because answers B and D happen between Brian's waking up and falling asleep; he doesn't fall asleep *first* after waking up.

B is correct because Brian hears mysterious sounds immediately upon waking up; in fact, the mysterious sounds are most likely what cause him to wake up in the first place.

C is incorrect because Brian notices his sunburn *before* waking up in the middle of the night.

D is incorrect because Brian first thinks the sounds are mysterious; it is later that he recognizes that an owl is making the sounds.

5

See answer key for sample response.

6

The first row should contain the following definition: "a journey." This is correct because the word *trip* is used to describe Fulton's journey by ship to Albany.

The second row should contain the following definition: "a group of things in the same category." This is correct because the word *kind* is used in the phrase "first trip of its kind"—meaning the first trip in a boat powered by a steam engine.

7

A is incorrect because the author does not explain Fulton's pricing decisions in the paragraph.

B is correct because the paragraph provides vivid examples of why the boat's sights and sounds scared potential passengers.

C is incorrect because the paragraph is not a technical explanation of how steam engines worked.

D is incorrect because the author does not provide information about consumers' feelings about prices.

8A

A is incorrect because, although sailing the river may have been dangerous, this is not the meaning of the word *unpredictable*.

B is incorrect because, although sailing the river may have been exhausting, this is not the meaning of the word *unpredictable*.

C is incorrect because "relaxing" is not the meaning of the word *unpredictable* and does not make sense in the context of the sentence.

D is correct because *unpredictable* means "difficult to predict," or "difficult to guess."

8B

A is correct because something that shifts is likely to be difficult to make predictions, or guesses, about.

B is incorrect because winds are not necessarily unpredictable; it's the fact that the winds shifted that made sailing the river unpredictable.

C is incorrect because tides on their own are not necessarily unpredictable; it's the fact that the tides shifted that made sailing the river unpredictable.

D is incorrect because rivers on their own are not necessarily unpredictable.

9A

A is incorrect because it is not the best summary of the author's point of view about Fulton's work.

B is correct because the author's main purpose throughout the text is to show that Fulton's work was important in helping popularize steamboat travel.

C is incorrect because the author does not compare Fulton's inventions to other people's inventions.

D is incorrect because the author never expresses the viewpoint that Fulton was more interested in money than public service.

9B

A is incorrect because this sentence simply describes the steamboat's chimney; it does not express the author's point of view.

B is incorrect because this sentence simply expresses the author's opinion of how the steamboat looked at night; it does not support the answer to part A.

C is incorrect because it simply states a fact about the trip; the sentence does not reveal the author's point of view about Fulton's work.

D is incorrect because the sentence does not describe Fulton's work.

E is correct because it expresses the author's point of view that Fulton's work helped popularize steamboat travel.

F is correct because it expresses the author's point of view that Fulton's work was a success, not something that should be criticized.

10

A is incorrect because both primary and secondary sources are likely to contain numbers.

B is incorrect because first-person reactions are a feature of primary sources, not secondary sources.

C is correct because only the author of a secondary source could have access to facts spanning more than 200 years culminating in "today."

D is incorrect because eyewitness opinions are a feature of primary sources.

11A

A is correct because the prefix *re-* suggests that the water bottle can be used "again."

B is incorrect because this answer does not relate to the prefix *re-*.

C is incorrect because this answer does not relate to the prefix *re-*.

D is incorrect because the text is focused on the primary use of water bottles.

11B

A is incorrect because the sentence does not hint at the meaning of *reusable*.

B is incorrect because the sentence does not relate to the idea of a *reusable* water bottle.

C is incorrect because the sentence points to Americans' wasteful plastic use, not the meaning of *reusable*.

D is correct because the sentence hints at the meaning of *reusable*; a reusable water bottle creates "no waste."

12

A is correct because the first paragraph—the introduction—clearly states the author's claim that using tap water instead of bottled water in schools will lead to greener and healthier schools.

B is incorrect because this idea is explained in the second paragraph.

C is incorrect because the author details how personal water bottles will make schools greener and healthier in the paragraphs that follow.

D is incorrect because the three areas are introduced in paragraphs 2 through 4.

13

A is incorrect because *show* is not a homograph that can mean "to be in charge or command of."

B is incorrect because *tap* is not a homograph that can mean "to be in charge or command of."

C is correct because *lead* is a homograph that can refer to a heavy metal or can mean "to be in charge or command of" when used as a verb.

D is incorrect because *can* is not a homograph that can mean "to be in charge or command of."

14A

A is incorrect because the graph makes no reference to how healthy tap water is.

B is incorrect because the graph does not have any information about landfills.

C is incorrect because the graph does not necessarily explain *why* Americans are buying more and more plastic water each year.

D is correct because the graph shows that Americans are buying more bottled water each year, which means more and more plastic waste.

14B

A is incorrect because the sentence does not relate to the idea that production of plastic waste is increasing in America.

B is incorrect because the sentence does not relate to the idea that production of plastic waste is increasing in America.

C is correct because the sentence supports the idea presented in the chart—that production of plastic waste is increasing in America.

D is incorrect because the sentence is about water waste, not plastic waste.

15

If students know they have constant access to tap water at school, they will likely bring fewer drinks from home (paragraph 2).

Because Americans are buying more and more bottled water every year, resources such as energy and landfill space are being stretched (paragraph 3).

If students have personal water bottles, they will have no reason to throw away water bottles; therefore, students will minimize water waste in their schools (paragraph 4).

16

A is incorrect because a coordinating conjunction following the comma is necessary when separating the two independent clauses.

B is incorrect because this sentence introduces an unnecessary comma and does not fix the original run-on sentence.

C is correct because the coordinating conjunction *and* (following a comma) is needed to form a grammatically correct compound sentence.

D is incorrect because the coordinating conjunction *but* shows an incorrect relationship between the two independent clauses.

17

A is incorrect because sentence 11 has only one verb.

B is incorrect because each subject in sentence 13 has only one verb.

C is incorrect because sentence 16 has only one verb.

D is correct because the verbs *found* and *made* share the same subject (*I*).

18

A is incorrect because it creates a run-on sentence.

B is incorrect because the conjunction *and,* though grammatically correct, does not fit the context as well as *but*.

C is incorrect because the conjunction *so* doesn't make sense in context.

D is correct because it creates a grammatically sound sentence and because the conjunction *but* correctly expresses the relationship between the two original sentences.

19

A is correct because it correctly sets off the dependent clause at the start of the complex sentence.

B is incorrect because it unnecessarily separates *Mom* from the narrator, and it doesn't correct the unnecessary repetition of *shopping.*

C is incorrect because the exclamation point is unnecessary, and the revision doesn't correct the unnecessary repetition of *shopping.*

D is incorrect because the semicolon unnecessarily separates *Mom* from the narrator, and the revision doesn't correct the unnecessary repetition of *shopping.*

20

A is incorrect because it creates a run-on, and it doesn't correct the missing comma after *daisies*.

B is incorrect because it creates a sentence fragment.

C is correct because *colorful daisies* is an item in a series and should be separated from the others with a comma.

D is incorrect because it uses punctuation incorrectly.

Unit Assessments

Unit 2 Answer Key   Student Name: _______________________

Question	Correct Answer	Content Focus	Complexity
1	A	Personification	DOK 2
2	C	Homographs	DOK 1
3	E, F	Theme	DOK 3
4	see below	Literary Elements: Setting	DOK 3
5A	A	Theme	DOK 3
5B	D	Theme / Text Evidence	DOK 2
6A	B	Context Clues	DOK 2
6B	D	Context Clues / Text Evidence	DOK 2
7	B, E	Text Features: Timelines	DOK 1
8	C	Text Structure: Problem and Solution	DOK 2
9	see below	Roots	DOK 2
10	see below	Text Structure: Problem and Solution	DOK 3
11A	D	Theme	DOK 3
11B	D	Theme / Textual Evidence	DOK 2
12	A	Literary Elements: Repetition	DOK 2
13	B	Personification	DOK 2
14	C, F	Literary Elements: Rhyme	DOK 2
15	see below	Theme	DOK 3
16	C	Prepositional Phrases	DOK 1
17	B	Prepositional Phrases	DOK 1
18	D	Singular and Plural Nouns	DOK 1
19	C	Kinds of Nouns	DOK 1
20	B	Possessive Nouns	DOK 1

Unit 2 Answer Key   Student Name: _______________________

Comprehension 3, 4, 5A, 5B, 7, 8, 10, 11A, 11B, 14, 15	/18	%
Vocabulary 1, 2, 6A, 6B, 9, 12, 13	/12	%
English Language Conventions 16, 17, 18, 19, 20	/5	%
Total Unit 2 Assessment Score	/35	%

4 Students should complete the chart as follows:

- kingdom with castle—It creates opportunity for Janko to work for a wealthy king and win his fortune
- forest—It creates opportunity for Janko to meet an old man, a raven, and a fish, which help him win his fortune
- set long ago, in a distant land—It creates opportunity for the main character to go on a quest and encounter magic
- large field—It creates opportunity for Janko to meet ants, which help him win his fortune

9 Students should write the following definitions in the chart:

- Row 1: possible
- Row 2: able to produce with little waste

10 **2-point response:** The people in Greensburg focused on rebuilding instead of giving up. When the tornado destroyed their town, the townspeople could have given up and moved someplace else, or they could have rebuilt everything the same way it was before. Instead, they decided to make something new and exciting. By working together, they rebuilt Greensburg as a "green" town. Their efforts resulted in safer and cleaner environments, employment opportunities, tourism, and pride in their town.

15 Students should match the following excerpts and answers:

- While the old Dutch clock in the chimney-place / Up with its hands before its face, / For it always dreaded a family row! — **B.** A clock always has "hands" on a "face," which suggests that the Dutch clock did not really have such a dramatic reaction.
- The Chinese plate looked very blue, / And wailed, "Oh, dear! what shall we do! — **A.** The Chinese plate's emotional response raises the level of drama surrounding the event.
- (*Don't fancy I exaggerate— / I got my news from the Chinese plate!*) — **B.** By having the speaker deny it, the author suggests that the speaker is, in fact, exaggerating.

Unit 2 Answer Key

Student Name: _______________________________

<table>
<tr><td colspan="4">Informational Performance Task</td></tr>
<tr><td>Question</td><td>Answer</td><td>Complexity</td><td>Score</td></tr>
<tr><td>1</td><td>see below</td><td>DOK 2</td><td>/1</td></tr>
<tr><td>2</td><td>see below</td><td>DOK 3</td><td>/2</td></tr>
<tr><td>3</td><td>see below</td><td>DOK 3</td><td>/2</td></tr>
<tr><td>Informational Article</td><td>see below</td><td>DOK 4</td><td>/4 [P/O]
/4 [E/E]
/2 [C]</td></tr>
<tr><td colspan="3">Total Score</td><td>/15</td></tr>
</table>

1   Students should match the following ideas and details:

- The earmuffs Chester patented were an improvement on what was available at the time.—"In order for you to patent your invention, it must be a new idea or it must be a big improvement on an old idea."
- Chester invented his earmuffs to solve a problem.—"However, people patent special types of wheels that they invent to solve problems."
- Chester started a company that made and sold his earmuffs.—"How can you make and sell your invention and make sure other companies don't make it too? You can apply for a patent."

2   **2-point response:** In Source #1, the reader is taken through the process of how George Nissen came up with, developed, and named his invention, the trampoline. Using information found in Source #3, the reader can understand the steps he needed to take to patent his invention and keep other people from using his idea. In Source #2, Chester Greenwood patented his improved earmuffs. Source #3 gives the rules for when inventions can be patented, letting the reader know that his ear muffs must have been considered a significant improvement on an old idea.

3   **2-point response:** People invent things because they see that there is a need for something new or because they see a way to make something better. In Source #1, George Nissen thought of a new gymnastics prop. He saw a need for the trampoline that most others could not see, and he spent much of his life helping others see its value. In Source #2, Chester Greenwood needed to find a way to protect his ears from the cold wind. This need led to an improvement in the ear muff important enough to patent.

10-point anchor paper: Have you ever thought you would like to be an inventor? Well, the first step is to come up with an idea for something new. It is also okay to come up with a big improvement on an old idea. Usually, inventions make life easier in some way. The inventions meet a need that people have.

The next step, of course, is to try building the invention if it is something that can be built. It is important to have a clear understanding of how the invention works. This is especially important if you intend to patent it. This is because you will have to show exactly what that would look like and how it will work.

Third, decide how you want to use your invention. If you want everyone to use it for free, then avoid getting a patent. If you want to make a company and earn money, it is probably a good idea to get a patent.

Next, do research to learn what similar things have been invented. This will help you avoid trying to get a patent for something that is already out there. It will also help you learn to describe what makes your invention unique. Finally, apply for the patent. Once your invention is patented, you can create a company that makes your invention available to many.

In Source #2, the reader can see most of this process in the context of Chester Greenwood's invention. He discovered a need, then thought of his invention. He made it with the help of his grandmother, patented it, and formed a company to make and sell his invention.

In Source #1, the reader can see other parts of the process emphasized. For example, George Nissen spent a great deal of energy creating a market for his invention. He needed to help the public see that his idea was a good one in order to be able to sell his invention. Both inventors went through a version of the process that I outline here. Both inventors follow roughly the same process, but it can look very different in different situations. What will you invent, and what will the process look like for you?

Unit Assessments

Unit 2 Rationales

1

A is correct because personification is the imbuing of nonhuman objects or animals with human qualities, such as speech—which the ant uses to thank Janko.

B is incorrect because the main conflict is between Janko and the king, two humans.

C is incorrect because the ant's ability to speak has nothing to do with the family's poverty.

D is incorrect because the ant's ability to speak helps to show the ant's kindness, not Janko's.

2

A is incorrect because this definition doesn't make sense in the context of the paragraph.

B is incorrect because *rose* is used as a verb in the sentence; this definition describes the homograph *rose* when used as a noun.

C is correct because *rose* is used to describe the sun at dawn; no other choice makes sense in context.

D is incorrect because this is a different definition of *rose* that does not make sense in the context of describing the sun.

3

A is incorrect because the sentence makes no reference to sharing a reward.

B is incorrect because the sentence is about how Janko helps the animals; it makes no reference to sharing a reward.

C is incorrect because the sentence makes no reference to sharing a reward.

D is incorrect because the sentence makes no reference to sharing a reward.

E is correct because the sentence recounts how Janko shares the wagons of gold with his family (after rejecting the king's offer of half his kingdom).

F is correct because the sentence recounts how Janko shares one of the wagons of gold with the man who advised him earlier.

4

First row: *set long ago, in a distant land.* This is correct because this aspect of the setting places the story in a time and place that is outside the real world we know.

Second row: *large field.* This is correct because Janko might not have finished his millet task without the help of the ants, and he might not have come upon ants without living near fields.

Third row: *forest.* This is correct because Janko might not have known where to find work and might not have rescued the princesses or found the ring without the help of the old man, the raven, and the fish. And he might not have come upon them without traveling through a forest.

Fourth row: *kingdom with a castle.* This is correct because Janko might not have found highly lucrative work without the presence of the king, and he would not have had access to a king if he did not live in a kingdom.

5A

A is correct because Janko's kindness toward animals is what allows him to succeed in his quest.

B is incorrect because the adventure itself does not bring Janko happiness.

C is incorrect because this theme is not expressed in the text, even though Janko spends time in nature.

D is incorrect because this theme is not supported by details in the text.

5B

A is incorrect because it only illustrates Janko's kindness, not the reward that kindness brings.

B is incorrect because it does not contain an example of kindness or reward.

C is incorrect because it does not contain an example of kindness or reward.

D is correct because it tells how the man's kind act of advising Janko results in the reward of a wagon full of gold.

6A

A is incorrect because *demolished* has a meaning that is almost the opposite of "avoided."

B is correct because *demolished* means "wrecked."

C is incorrect because *demolished* has a stronger, more negative meaning than "affected."

D is incorrect because *demolished* has a different meaning than "involved."

6B

A is incorrect because this clue does not hint at the meaning of *demolished*.

B is incorrect because this clue on its own does not hint at the meaning of *demolished*.

C is incorrect because this clue on its own does not hint at the meaning of *demolished*.

D is correct because the clue "destroyed or badly damaged" shows that *demolished* means "wrecked."

7

A is incorrect because this information is included in the text only, not in the time line.

B is correct because the time line shows that the residents received an emergency message that the tornado was headed to Greensburg at 9:35, only ten minutes before the tornado hit.

C is incorrect because this information is included in the text only, not in the time line.

D is incorrect because this information is included in the text only, not in the time line.

E is correct because the time line shows that the National Weather Service issued a warning about a tornado in a nearby county at 8:55.

F is incorrect because the people of Greensburg did receive a warning close to the time that the tornado entered the town.

8

A is incorrect because the author does not compare the population of Greensburg before and after the hurricane.

B is incorrect because the author does not mention how the town intends to protect against future tornadoes.

C is correct because the author explains how Greensburg rebuilt as a "green" town that attracted tourists.

D is incorrect because the detail about a new school and hospital is not the best way to describe how Greensburg recovered from the tornado.

9

First row: "possible" is the correct meaning of the word *potential* in the context of the sentence. The meaning of the root *potis* ("capable") points to this definition.

Second row: "able to produce with little waste" is the correct meaning of the word *efficient* in the context of the sentence. The meaning of the root *fic* ("make") hints at this definition.

10

See answer key for sample response.

11A

A is incorrect because no connection to human behavior is stated or implied in the poem.

B is incorrect because the poem provides no evidence that the characters have no control over their actions.

C is incorrect because the poem provides no evidence that the dog and cat were ever best friends.

D is correct because the speaker is basing the story on secondhand information from the clock, the plate, and what "some folks" think—thus casting doubt on the truth of the story.

11B

A is incorrect because these lines do not show that that the speaker is receiving secondhand information.

B is incorrect because these lines do not show that that the speaker is receiving secondhand information.

C is incorrect because these lines do not show that that the speaker is receiving secondhand information.

D is correct because these lines discuss how the speaker's opinion differs from that of "some folks"—and that, in each case, those opinions are based on secondhand information.

12

A is correct because the repeated references to bits of gingham and calico flying around create a strong visual image of the animals' duel.

B is incorrect because the animals' cloth patterns are not relevant to the meaning of the poem.

C is incorrect because the author never places a value judgment on the animals' appearance, so the reader learns nothing about the animals' appeal for a burglar.

D is incorrect because the word *calico* appears at the end of a line only once, and no line ends with *gingham*.

13

A is incorrect because personification is unrelated to foreshadowing generally, as well as in this poem; the fact that the clock and the plate are given human qualities does not in itself indicate how the story will end.

B is correct because the author personifies the clock, plate, and stuffed animals by giving them the abilities to speak and to feel, thus turning them into characters in the story.

C is incorrect because the author does not compare the dog and the cat in this poem.

D is incorrect because the author does not create tension between the speaker and the animals; the animals appear to be unaware of the speaker.

14

A is incorrect because the rhyme scheme alone has no impact on how readers perceive the clock and the plate.

B is incorrect because the rhyme scheme does not make the events in the poem any more or less believable.

C is correct because the sing-song quality of the regular rhyme scheme softens the topic of a violent fight between two stuffed animals.

D is incorrect because important words are scattered throughout the poem; they are not limited to rhyming words.

E is incorrect because the rhyme scheme affects the rhythm; the descriptive words the poet uses help the reader visualize the setting.

F is correct because the rhyming lines help emphasize the poem's rhythm and sing-song quality.

15

The line "While the old Dutch clock in the chimney-place / Up with its hands before its face, / For it always dreaded a family row!" uses puns ("hands" and "face" each have two meanings) to suggest that the Dutch clock did not really react in such a dramatic way.

The line "The Chinese plate looked very blue / And wailed, 'Oh, dear! What shall we do!'" also shows the plate's overdramatic reaction to the fight between the dog and cat.

The line *"(Don't fancy I exaggerate— / I got my news from the Chinese plate!)"* supports the theme by suggesting that the speaker is exaggerating, or stretching the truth.

   Unit Assessments

16

A is incorrect because the phrase does not contain a preposition.

B is incorrect because the phrase does not contain a preposition.

C is correct because "on their backs" is a prepositional phrase that begins with the preposition "on."

D is incorrect because the word "as" is used as a conjunction in sentence 1.

17

A is incorrect because the prepositional phrase is "behind the woodstove," which does not show how the chipmunk ran.

B is correct because the prepositional phrase is "behind the woodstove," which explains where the chipmunk hid.

C is incorrect because the prepositional phrase is "behind the woodstove," which does not explain where the stove is.

D is incorrect because the prepositional phrase is "behind the woodstove," which does not describe the stove.

18

A is incorrect because the sentence uses the incorrect form of the plural noun *people*; the noun should not be possessive.

B is incorrect because the sentence uses the incorrect form of the plural noun *people*; the noun should not be possessive.

C is incorrect because *people* is a plural noun and requires a plural verb.

D is correct because *people* is the correct form of the noun; it's a plural noun and takes a plural verb, *were*.

19

A is incorrect because none of the nouns in sentence 9 are abstract.

B is incorrect because none of the nouns in sentence 10 are abstract.

C is correct because the word *protection* is an abstract noun—it is a noun that cannot be seen, felt, smelled, heard, or touched.

D is incorrect because none of the nouns in sentence 13 are abstract.

20

A is incorrect because the sentence uses the incorrect form of the possessive plural noun *chipmunks'*.

B is correct because the sentence uses the correct form of the possessive plural noun *chipmunks'*.

C is incorrect because the sentence uses the incorrect form of the possessive plural noun *chipmunks'*.

D is incorrect because the sentence uses the incorrect form of the possessive plural noun *chipmunks'*.

Unit 3 Answer Key   Student Name: _______________________

Question	Correct Answer	Content Focus	Complexity
1	C	Figurative Language	DOK 2
2	see below	Text Features: Dialogue	DOK 2
3A	D	Theme	DOK 3
3B	D	Theme / Text Evidence	DOK 2
4	D	Theme	DOK 3
5A	C	Context Clues: Cause and Effect	DOK 2
5B	B, F	Context Clues: Cause and Effect / Text Evidence	DOK 2
6	B	Author's Point of View	DOK 2
7A	C	Context Clues: Sentence Clues	DOK 2
7B	A	Context Clues: Sentence Clues / Text Evidence	DOK 2
8	D, E	Context Clues: Sentence Clues	DOK 2
9	see below	Main Idea and Key Details	DOK 2
10	see below	Author's Purpose	DOK 2
11A	A	Author's Point of View	DOK 3
11B	C	Author's Point of View / Text Evidence	DOK 2
12	C	Context Clues: Sentence Clues	DOK 2
13	see below	Main Idea and Key Details	DOK 2
14	D	Latin Roots	DOK 1
15	A, B	Text Structure: Problem and Solution	DOK 2
16	B	Avoid Shifting Tenses	DOK 1
17	C	Verb Tenses	DOK 1
18	A	Subject-Verb Agreement	DOK 1
19	D	Main and Helping Verbs	DOK 1
20	B	Contractions	DOK 1

          Unit Assessments

Unit 3 Answer Key   Student Name: _______________________

Comprehension 2, 3A, 3B, 4, 6, 9, 10, 11A, 11B, 13, 15	/18	%
Vocabulary 1, 5A, 5B, 7A, 7B, 8, 12, 14	/12	%
English Language Conventions 16, 17, 18, 19, 20	/5	%
Total Unit 3 Assessment Score	/35	%

2 Students should complete the chart as follows:
- "Josh, you see Ethan every day. You need to spend some time with your grandfather," Mom answered with a stern look. (Mom)—is dedicated to family
- "But, Mom," I whined, "he never wants to do anything interesting." (Josh)—has a desire to be entertained
- "This is foxglove," he continued, gesturing to a delicate, bell-shaped flower, "which is used to make something called *digitalis*, a medicine for people with heart disease." (Grandpa)—has a lot of knowledge
- "Could we find some more plants?" I asked. (Josh)—is curious

9 Students should circle the following:
- Main Idea: snow globes were discovered accidentally
- Detail: "because of an experiment that did not work"

10 **2-point response:** The author most likely wanted to show how Erwin Perzy is someone to admire. When Perzy got a new idea, he worked hard and kept trying. For example, he encountered many setbacks with glitter and powder falling to the bottom of his glass globe. But he never gave up. When he solved his problem, he patented the snow globe. Eventually he formed a large company that still exists today.

13 Students should complete the chart with the following sentences:
- Main Idea: Coding skills are an essential part of modern literacy.
- Key detail: Coding helps kids understand their world and be powerful within it.
- Key detail: The "language" of code is all around kids.
- Key detail: Coding includes many other helpful skills.

Unit 3 Answer Key   Student Name: _______________________

Opinion Performance Task			
Question	**Answer**	**Complexity**	**Score**
1	see below	DOK 2	/1
2	see below	DOK 3	/2
3	see below	DOK 3	/2
Opinion Essay	see below	DOK 4	/4 [P/O] /4 [E/E] /2 [C]
Total Score			**/15**

1   Students should match the following:
   • Source #2: Queen bees lay their eggs in the brood chamber of the hive.
   • Source #3: Bees send out scouts to look for a place to build a new hive.

2   **2-point response:** Source #1 explains the health benefits of honey. These include aiding digestion, increasing calcium absorption, calming coughs, and healing scrapes. Source # 2 explains the ease and popularity of caring for honeybees. Source #3 explains that honeybees produce valuable honey and help plants grow through pollination.

3   **2-point response:** Bees are valuable to people for many reasons. Source #1 explains a number of reasons why the honey produced by honeybees is beneficial. For example, scientists are studying honey and its ability to kill germs and assist people with allergies. Source #3 explains that bees are valuable because they are responsible for spreading the pollen that helps plants grow. Today honeybees help pollinate about 100 food crops in the United States.

10-point anchor paper: Last year, I walked too close to a beehive and the bees in the hive swarmed down on me. I was stung several times. Ever since that time, I have been terrified of bees. If this company's plan to make beekeepers of my classmates becomes real, I will have a problem. I will have to learn to swallow my fear, and everyone else like me will have to do the same. I want to help stop this idea before it goes any further.

I realize that bees make honey, the "golden treasure," as the author of Source #1 calls it. I like honey, and I also realize that it has many important health benefits. For one thing, honey seems to protect people from allergies. "Honeybees are valuable insects," the author of Source #3 writes, but the same author also writes, "bees near homes can become a nuisance."

The problem is that putting a beehive in our school can create a problem for everyone in the school. After flowers stop blooming in the late summer, the bees look for other kinds of food than nectar and pollen. The author of Source #3 states that sweet "treats such as juices, sugar, and fruits attract" bees. This means that if the bees cannot find what they need, they could fly all around the school looking for food in garbage containers and even in leftover cans and bottles.

Late spring is another problem season. Bees from one nest will leave to look for a place to build a new nest. According to Source #3, they will sometimes look for cracks in the walls of buildings to build a nest. I do not blame the bees for this, but I don't want them nesting all over the school.

As the author of Source #2 shows, beekeeping can be an interesting hobby. People get to watch all the life stages of bees. I would try it myself if bees did not sting. Unfortunately, bees do sting, and they terrify some people, like me. Before the school board decides to invite thousands of new bees into our school, it should think hard about how this decision will affect everyone in the school.

Unit 3 Rationales

1

A is incorrect because nothing in the story suggests that Grandpa is confused.

B is incorrect because the narrator explains in the sentence that Grandpa examines plants, not animals.

C is correct because Grandpa is described as "darting from place to place" to explore the plants, and jackrabbits are known to move quickly.

D is incorrect because there is no sense anywhere in the text that Grandpa is "overwhelmed."

2

Mom's insistence that Josh spend time with Grandpa shows that she places a high importance on family interaction.

Josh's critical comment that Grandpa "never wants to do anything interesting" shows that he wants someone or something to entertain him.

Grandpa indicates that he is highly knowledgeable about woodland plants and their uses.

Josh's eagerness to explore further at the end of the text shows that he is curious to learn more and able to change his former attitude.

3A

A is incorrect because the text does not involve anyone getting into trouble.

B is incorrect because the text emphasizes how Josh can get along with his grandfather too, not just his peers.

C is incorrect because the woods in the text are portrayed as fascinating and educational, not dark and mysterious.

D is correct because the events in the text, as well as Josh's changing attitude, show that an elderly man who appears boring to a kid actually has passions and knowledge that anyone could find valuable and exciting.

3B

A is incorrect because this excerpt shows Josh's behavior in the beginning—before he realizes that his grandpa has something special to offer.

B is incorrect because this excerpt does not support the theme that everyone has something special to offer.

C is incorrect because it is not the best example to support the theme that everyone has something special to offer.

D is correct because it shows Josh coming to the realization that his grandfather has something special to offer.

4

A is incorrect because this sentence makes no reference to treating blackberries with respect and caution.

B is incorrect because this sentence makes no reference to treating an aspect of nature with caution.

C is incorrect because this sentence makes no reference to treating foxglove with caution.

D is correct because this reference to foxglove shows that people should be cautious about consuming foxglove, which (as the previous sentence reveals) should also be respected because it is used to treat heart disease.

5A

A is incorrect because "tasty" is not the definition of *edible*.

B is incorrect because "pretty to see" is not the definition of *edible* and does not fit the context of the sentence.

C is correct because "safe to eat" is the definition of *edible*.

D is incorrect because "well known" is not the definition of *edible* and does not fit the context of the sentence.

5B

A is incorrect "starting to get interested" does not hint at the meaning of *edible*.

B is correct because Grandpa says that "not all plants are edible" after Josh asks what other plants "could be eaten," which suggests that "could be eaten" relates to the meaning of *edible*.

C is incorrect because "my stomach growling" suggests that Josh is hungry, but the phrase is not one of the two best context clues that help the reader understand that *edible* means "safe to eat."

D is incorrect because "all around you" does not hint at the meaning of *edible*.

E is incorrect because the phrase "not all plants" on its own does not hint at the meaning of *edible*.

F is correct because Grandpa relates the word *edible* to something that does or does not make you sick when you eat it.

6

A is incorrect because the author never suggests that Perzy was not skilled in using electricity; the author only mentions that the newly invented electric light bulb "created adequate light."

B is correct because the author explains how when Perzy's "experiment failed again . . . it sparked a new idea."

C is incorrect because the author never calls Perzy's creativity into question.

D is incorrect because the author explains that Perzy's job was to make surgical tools, not that he was "mainly interested in them."

Unit Assessments

7A

A is incorrect because "changed around" is not the meaning of *contemplated*.

B is incorrect because "solved quickly" is not the meaning of *contemplated*.

C is correct because *contemplated* means "thought about."

D is incorrect because "worried over" is not the meaning of *contemplated*.

7B

A is correct because the word "remembered" suggests that *contemplated* means "thought about."

B is incorrect because the word "special" does not hint at the meaning of *contemplated*.

C is incorrect because the word "trick" does not hint at the meaning of *contemplated*.

D is incorrect because the word "candles" does not hint at the meaning of *contemplated*.

8

A is incorrect because the word "metal" describes the material of the structure, rather than the meaning of *structure*.

B is incorrect because the word "pewter" describes the material of the structure, rather than the meaning of *structure*.

C is incorrect because the word "workshop" describes where Perzy made the structure; it does not help define the meaning of *structure*.

D is correct because the word "model" helps to explain that Perzy made a small version of a famous *structure*, or construction.

E is correct because the word "building" helps to explain that a *structure* is a construction, or building.

F is incorrect because the word "snow" describes the environment around the structure.

9

The main idea of the text is that "snow globes were discovered accidentally" because the author focuses on how Perzy came to invent snow globes by accident.

The detail that best supports the main idea is "because of an experiment that did not work," which explains how Perzy got the idea for snow globes.

10

See answer key for sample response.

11A

A is correct because the author argues that coding helps kids "hand[le] frustration" and become "confident" and "enthusiastic."

B is incorrect because the author never expresses this point of view.

C is incorrect because the author never expresses this point of view.

D is incorrect because the author says that coding can help someone get certain jobs, not that it is necessary.

11B

A is incorrect because the sentence does not address how coding can have a positive effect on kids' emotions.

B is incorrect because it addresses career benefits rather than emotional ones.

C is correct because it supports the author's point of view that learning how to code has several emotional benefits, such as a feeling of "wide-open" freedom, personal expression, confidence, enthusiasm, and empowerment.

D is incorrect because it does not directly support the author's point about emotional benefits.

12

A is incorrect because the word "creating" can apply to multiple types of machines; this word bears no inherent relationship to the meaning of *digital*.

B is incorrect because the fact that there are multiple commands bears no inherent relationship to the meaning of *digital*.

C is correct because computers and smartphones are examples of digital technology, and readers are likely to know this.

D is incorrect because commands—instructions on "what to do"—can exist in any context, digital or otherwise.

13

"Coding skills are an essential part of modern literacy" best states the main idea of the passage (and summarizes the topic sentence). The best three key supporting details are "The 'language' of code is all around kids" (sentence 6), "Coding helps kids understand their world and be powerful within it" (sentence 5), and "Coding includes many other helpful skills" (sentence 1).

The sentence "Problems are called 'bugs' in coding language" is a small detail in paragraph 2, not a key detail. The sentence "Coding can be a frustrating activity" misinterprets information given in paragraph 2 (that coding can help students handle frustration).

14

A is incorrect because the Latin root *cred* suggests nothing about punctuality.

B is incorrect because the Latin root *cred* suggests nothing about being a good writer.

C is incorrect because the Latin root *cred* suggests nothing about being one of the best students; someone can have the right credentials and still not be "one of the top students."

D is correct because the Latin root *cred* suggests that credentials make a job candidate believable or trustworthy.

15

A is correct because the sentence explains the cause-and-effect relationship of consuming technology: when we consume, or use, technology, we are not always fully engaged.

B is correct because the author explains that learning how to code can help kids learn how to handle frustration.

C is incorrect because the author never suggests that learning coding will qualify someone in the field of sales.

D is incorrect because the author states that "playing a game" is just one example of ways that we consume technology.

E is incorrect because public speaking does not relate that closely to any of the skills that the author says coding would help sharpen.

F is incorrect because learning how to code will not help students read more for pleasure.

16

A is incorrect because it introduces an unnecessary comma and doesn't correct the tense shift and error in subject-verb agreement.

B is correct because it brings the verb tense back to the present, which should be consistent.

C is incorrect because the answer maintains the incorrect shift from present to past tense and introduces a usage error with the contraction *it's*.

D is incorrect because it doesn't correct the tense shift; the authors should stick to the present tense.

17

A is incorrect because it introduces a new verb tense error; the sentence requires the future tense.

B is incorrect because it does not correct the verb tense error.

C is correct because it changes the verb to the correct tense: future.

D is incorrect because the sentence contains a verb tense error; the sentence requires the future tense.

18

A is correct because it fixes the error in subject-verb agreement; the collective noun *team* should take the singular verb *has*, even though it is separated by the propositional phrase "of experts."

B is incorrect because the sentence introduces an error with the prepositional phrase "team of experts."

C is incorrect because the sentence does not fix the error in subject-verb agreement and introduces an error with the prepositional phrase "team of experts."

D is incorrect because the sentence introduces an error with the prepositional phrase "team of experts."

19

A is incorrect because sentence 1 does not contain a helping verb.

B is incorrect because sentence 3 does not contain a helping verb.

C is incorrect because sentence 7 does not contain a helping verb.

D is correct because sentence 10 contains the helping verb *will*.

20

A is incorrect because the sentence misuses the contraction *you're*; the sentence requires a possessive pronoun.

B is correct because the sentence correctly spells the possessive pronoun *your* and correctly places the apostrophe after the "n" in *aren't* to show the contraction for *are not*.

C is incorrect because the sentence does not fix the apostrophe error in *are'nt*.

D is incorrect because the word *That's* should include an apostrophe to show that it is a contraction for *That is*.

Unit Assessments

Unit 4 Answer Key   Student Name: ___________________

Question	Correct Answer	Content Focus	Complexity
1	B	Structural Elements of Drama	DOK 2
2	see below	Adages and Proverbs	DOK 2
3A	A	Theme	DOK 3
3B	C	Theme / Text Evidence	DOK 2
4	E, F	Simile and Metaphor	DOK 2
5	see below	Point of View	DOK 2
6	see below	Prefixes and Suffixes	DOK 2
7	B, C, D	Author's Point of View	DOK 2
8	D	Prefixes and Suffixes	DOK 2
9	D	Figurative Language	DOK 3
10A	B	Author's Point of View	DOK 2
10B	D	Author's Point of View / Text Evidence	DOK 2
11	A	Simile and Metaphor	DOK 2
12A	A	Point of View	DOK 2
12B	C	Point of View / Text Evidence	DOK 2
13	C, E	Simile and Metaphor	DOK 2
14	see below	Theme	DOK 3
15	A	Figurative Language	DOK 2
16	D	Pronouns and Antecedents	DOK 1
17	C	Pronouns and Homophones	DOK 1
18	A	Kinds of Pronouns	DOK 1
19	B	Possessive Pronouns	DOK 1
20	B	Reflexive Pronouns	DOK 1

Unit 4 Answer Key   Student Name: _______________________

Comprehension 1, 3A, 3B, 5, 7, 9, 10A, 10B, 12A, 12B, 14, 15	/18	%
Vocabulary 2, 4, 6, 8, 11, 13	/12	%
English Language Conventions 16, 17, 18, 19, 20	/5	%
Total Unit 4 Assessment Score	/35	%

2 Students should match the following adages and meanings:

- "out of the frying pan into the fire"—going from a difficult situation to an even worse one
- "the hour is darkest before the dawn"—just when things seem to be at their worst, they get better

5 **2-point response:** Wheatley respects Washington because of his achievements. She tells him that she agrees with the view of the American people that he is a good leader. She says that his "bravery, honesty, manners, intelligence—are well known." Wheatley expresses this view in the poem she published. In the poem, she calls Washington "His Excellency."

6 Students should complete the chart as follows:

- activist—a person who campaigns to bring about social change
- reform—to make changes in something in order to improve it
- supporter—a person who encourages someone or something
- unfairly—in a way that does not follow the principles of equality and justice

14 Students should complete the chart as follows:

- Theme 1: Imagination brings us comfort—The speaker thinks of the daffodils when he is feeling sad.
- Theme 2: Nature brings us joy.—The speaker cannot stop looking at the field.

       Unit Assessments

Unit 4 Answer Key   Student Name: _______________________

Narrative Performance Task			
Question	Answer	Complexity	Score
1	B, D	DOK 2	/1
2	see below	DOK 3	/2
3	see below	DOK 3	/2
Story	see below	DOK 4	/4 [P/O] /4 [D/E] /2 [C]
Total Score			/15

2   **2-point response:** Source #1 discusses Braille, a system using raised dots to represent letters. This form of communication allows people who are blind to use their fingertips to learn information from books and to communicate in written form. Source #2 describes an alphabet that was developed using pictures to represent the sounds and syllables of the Cherokee language. In the past, the Cherokee people were only able to communicate verbally. This new development allowed them to communicate using written language.

3   **2-point response:** In Source #1, Louis Braille set out to develop a better way for blind people to communicate through writing. He spent many years trying to develop a system that was easy to use and to understand. His first attempt, using "night-writing," was difficult to read and confusing. However, because he never gave up, people with sight disabilities today can communicate using the Braille system that he developed.

In Source #2, Sequoyah wished to give the Cherokee people a way to communicate with others and to record their history. His initial attempt at using symbols to represent Cherokee words ended in failure. Even when his friends told him to, he refused to give up on his idea. Eventually, his efforts led to the development of the first Native-American newspaper.

10-point anchor paper: I was sitting at my desk, waiting for the bell to ring when I noticed a girl with long blonde hair standing in the doorway. Glancing at her, I recalled seeing her picture in the local paper. She was the daughter of a visiting musician from Russia who was spending the next year working at the university. I smiled and waved. It must be frightening to walk into a room filled with strangers. She smiled back and walked toward me.

"Hi! Would you like to sit beside me? Here is an empty desk." I offered. "My name is Sally. I read about your family in the newspaper last week," I said slowly and clearly.

She just smiled in return.

Deciding that I needed to try something different, I took a piece of paper and wrote my name, adding an arrow beside it that pointed at me. She responded by taking out a pencil, writing a word, and drawing an arrow too.

"It is nice to meet you, Alina!" I said.

Science class began when Mr. Schuester walked into the classroom. He noticed that Alina was sitting in the vacant chair, so he asked her if she would like to introduce herself to the class. Smiling, she walked to the front of the room, carrying the piece of paper. She held it up and said, "Alina."

Mr. Schuester recognized that Alina did not speak English. He called the office to get help. Soon Mrs. Johansen, an English as a Second Language teacher, arrived in our classroom. Mrs. Johansen is my mom's best friend, so I told her what I read in the newspaper.

"I think that your attempt to be friends with Alina will be very helpful, Sally. She knows that you will do whatever it takes to communicate with her. Would you like to be her language mentor?" Mrs. Johansen asked.

"Sure," I agreed.

Alina and I worked together during study hall and after school. We practiced with flash cards and with programs on the computer. Sometimes we even listened to children's nursery songs in her language so that she could practice translating them into English.

Weeks and months flew by. Without even working hard, I had managed to learn Russian while teaching Alina my language. We both laughed when I told Alina that I had even had a dream where everyone was speaking in Russian!

When Alina's father's position at the university ended, we were quite sad. We made a promise to video chat every week so that we could practice our new language skills. We also decided to email each other in the language we were learning. We wanted to keep our friendship alive and build our language skills.

Three years have passed, and we still continue our weekly video chats in both languages. My best friend may be thousands of miles away from me, but technology keeps us close.

Unit 4 Rationales

1

A is incorrect because the stage directions in Scene 2 introduce the flashback; Scene 3 jumps back to 1776.

B is correct because the stage directions explain Wheatley's entrance to the room, as well as where both characters are situated as they speak to each other.

C is incorrect because there is no evidence that this is the function of the stage directions.

D is incorrect because the characters were explained in Scene 1 and Wheatley (as a child) was introduced in Scene 2.

2

The proverb "Out of the frying pan into the fire" means "going from a difficult situation to an even worse one." Washington is explaining how the people might at first feel relief at leaving a difficult situation (the frying pan) but later feel that the next situation is even worse (the fire).

The proverb "the hour is darkest before the dawn" means "just when things seem to be at their worst, they get better." Wheatley uses the proverb to encourage Washington to have hope.

3A

A is correct because, despite her difficult position in life, Wheatley achieved many accomplishments, and at the end of the play, Washington finds encouragement from her life story to stay positive in his struggle against England.

B is incorrect because the interpretation does not make sense; no characters behaved strangely in this play.

C is incorrect because there is no evidence that either character was disappointed with the meeting.

D is incorrect because trust is not an important idea in the play, and the relationship between Wheatley and Washington is not necessarily a friendship.

3B

A is incorrect because the line shows that Phillis Wheatley seemed intelligent when she was a baby, before she accomplished things.

B is incorrect because the line is not the best example of succeeding against all odds.

C is correct because the line shows Wheatley's amazing accomplishment—that she published a book despite the odds stacked against her.

D is incorrect because the line is more about having hope than succeeding against all odds.

4

A is incorrect because the statement does not relate to the idea that Wheatley was a gifted poet, or "favored by the muses."

B is incorrect because the statement does not relate to the idea that Wheatley was a gifted poet, or "favored by the muses."

C is incorrect because the statement does not relate to the idea that Wheatley was a gifted poet, or "favored by the muses."

D is incorrect because the statement does not relate to the idea that Wheatley was a gifted poet, or "favored by the muses."

E is correct because the statement shows that Wheatley had an interest in poetry when she was young, which would help her become a gifted poet, or "favored by the muses."

F is correct because the statement shows that Wheatley was a gifted poet, or "favored by the muses."

5

See answer key for sample response.

6

Activist is the correct answer for row 1 because the suffix *-ist* means "not" and the suffix *-able* means "can be."

Reform is the correct answer for row 2 because the prefix *re-* means "again"; the word *reform* therefore means "form again," or "to make changes in something to improve it."

Supporter is the correct answer for row 3 because the suffix *-er* means "one who does something"; the word *supporter* therefore means "one who supports or encourages."

Unfairly is the correct answer for row 4 because the prefix *-un* means "not"; the word *unfairly* therefore means "in a way that is not fair."

The other two words are incorrect. *Amendment* relates to "mak[ing] changes in something in order to improve it," but it is a noun, not a verb. *Involved* is too general to match any of the definitions in the chart.

7

A is incorrect because the simple fact that Anthony grew up with seven siblings did not influence her to fight for equal rights.

B is correct because the values Anthony's family taught her helped influence her to fight for equal rights.

C is correct because being surrounded by other anti-slavery activists inspired Anthony to act as well.

D is correct because the text states that the experience of not being allowed to give a speech "pushed her to work toward equal rights for women, including suffrage, or the right to vote."

E is incorrect because, although Stanton may have influenced Anthony, the fact that Stanton wrote most of her speeches did not influence Anthony to fight for equal rights.

F is incorrect because Anthony's refusal to pay a fine for voting would not have influenced her to fight for equal rights.

G is incorrect because Anthony's experiences giving speeches are examples of her fight for equal rights, not experiences that influenced her to fight for equal rights.

   Unit Assessments

8

A is incorrect because the suffix *-less* does not mean "one who does something."

B is incorrect because the suffix *-less* does not mean "the state of."

C is incorrect because this meaning suggests the opposite meaning of *tireless*.

D is correct because the suffix *-less* means "without," so *tireless* refers to a prolonged effort.

9

A is incorrect because the amendment finally passed fourteen years after Anthony's death.

B is incorrect because the phrase "paved the road" is used figuratively; Anthony did not actually work in construction.

C is incorrect because Congress did not agree with Anthony any of the times she asked Congress for equal rights.

D is correct because phrase "paved the road" is used figuratively to explain that Anthony's work was instrumental in the amendment eventually passing years after her death.

10A

A is incorrect because the sentence is not entirely true: Anthony did not live to see her dream of women's suffrage realized.

B is correct because the author begins the passage by stating that "Anthony spent her entire life trying to bring positive change to American society."

C is incorrect because the author does not claim that Anthony was unsuccessful without Stanton.

D is incorrect because, even though the author does suggest this idea, it does not represent his or her overall point of view on Anthony.

10B

A is incorrect because the sentence does not relate to Anthony's "lifelong effort to improve Americans' lives."

B is incorrect because the sentence refers to two examples of Anthony's work rather than her "lifelong effort to improve Americans' lives."

C is incorrect because the sentence refers to only one example of Anthony's "lifelong effort to improve Americans' lives."

D is correct because the sentence best summarizes Anthony's "lifelong effort to improve Americans' lives."

11

A is correct because the speaker uses a simile to compare himself to a lonely cloud; the daffodils brighten his mood.

B is incorrect because the speaker compares his loneliness to that of a cloud; the speaker is not actually a cloud.

C is incorrect because the speaker compares his loneliness to that of a cloud; he does not only feel gloomy on cloudy days.

D is incorrect because the speaker never mentions feeling comfortable being alone; he feels "lonely as a cloud."

12A

A is correct because the speaker says that the daffodils "outdid the sparkling waves in glee."

B is incorrect because there is no indication in the poem that the speaker thinks there are *too* many daffodils, just that there are many of them.

C is incorrect because there is no indication in the poem that the speaker is overwhelmed by the ocean; the speaker only mentions that the sparkling waves danced.

D is incorrect because the speaker mentions that he thinks about the daffodils when he is feeling lonely.

12B

A is incorrect because the lines show that there are many daffodils, not that they look joyful.

B is incorrect because the lines describe the dancing daffodils but don't necessarily show that they look joyful.

C is correct because the speaker explains in these lines that the daffodils "outdid the sparkling waves in glee."

D is incorrect because the lines explain how the speaker thinks of the daffodils when he is feeling lonely, not that they look joyful.

13

A is incorrect because the speaker uses the word *continuous* to describe the great number of daffodils, not how bright they are.

B is incorrect because the speaker says the daffodils are "continuous as stars" to explain that there are a lot of them, not that they are far away.

C is correct because the word *continuous* gives a clue that the speaker is comparing the great number of daffodils to the great number of stars in the sky.

D is incorrect because the word *continuous* helps to show that the speaker is comparing the number of daffodils and stars, not individual sizes.

E is correct because the speaker says in line 6 that the daffodils are "fluttering," much like the stars that "twinkle on the milky way."

F is incorrect because the word *continuous* helps to show that the speaker is comparing the number of daffodils and stars, not that the daffodils can only be seen by moonlight.

14

The theme "Imagination brings us comfort" is supported by the detail that the speaker pictures the daffodils dancing. Suddenly, he is no longer "lonely as a cloud" because he is surrounded by dancers in his imagination. The memory of the moment comes back to comfort him later in solemn moments.

The theme "Being in nature brings us joy" is supported by the detail that the speaker cannot stop gazing at the daffodils. Gazing at them brings the speaker joy, but only later does he realize that the daffodils can also bring comfort in times of loneliness.

   Unit Assessments

15

A is correct because the speaker feels happy when he remembers the daffodils in the field.

B is incorrect because nothing suggests that the speaker wants to be a daffodil.

C is incorrect because, although the speaker remembers the daffodils dancing, he does not indicate that he sees them wherever he goes.

D is incorrect because the speaker thinks of the daffodils dancing; he does not dance along with them.

16

A is incorrect because the pronoun at the start of the sentence (*It*) should refer back to *He and his family* in the previous sentence.

B is incorrect because the pronoun at the start of the sentence (*He*) should refer back to *He and his family* in the previous sentence; the second pronoun, *they*, is also incorrect because it should describe Armstrong only, not the family.

C is incorrect because the sentence mistakenly uses the object pronoun *him*.

D is correct because *They* clearly refers back to *family* in the previous sentence; the sentence also uses *Armstrong* to make it clear that he is the one who finished high school, not the entire family.

17

A is incorrect because it introduces the wrong relative pronoun (*which*) and does not fix the misuse of *they're*.

B is incorrect because it introduces an error (*pilot's* should remain as a singular possessive noun) and does not fix the misuse of *they're*.

C is correct because the sentence uses the plural possessive pronoun *their*.

D is incorrect because the sentence mistakenly uses the word *there* instead of the correct possessive pronoun *their*.

18

A is correct because it uses the relative pronoun *that* to refer to *organization* (a thing) instead of *who*, which is used with people.

B is incorrect because the relative pronoun *whom* is used with people (and is an object pronoun), but the pronoun refers to *organization*, which is a thing.

C is incorrect because the relative pronoun *whose* is used with people, but the pronoun refers to *organization*, which is a thing.

D is incorrect because the sentence uses a nonessential clause (introduced by a comma); the clause is essential in describing *organization*.

19

A is incorrect because the possessive pronoun's antecedent is *He,* so the possessive pronoun should refer to Armstrong only.

B is correct because the pronoun's antecedent is *He,* so the possessive pronoun should be *his.*

C is incorrect because the possessive pronoun's antecedent is *He,* so the possessive pronoun should refer to Armstrong.

D is incorrect because the sentence has an error in pronoun-antecedent agreement.

20

A is incorrect because *this* correctly refers to the Apollo 11 mission; the sentence contains an error with the reflexive pronoun.

B is correct because *hisself* is an incorrect spelling of the reflexive pronoun *himself.*

C is incorrect because it introduces an unnecessary comma and does not fix the incorrect spelling of the reflexive pronoun *himself.*

D is incorrect because the possessive pronoun *its* is needed in this usage, not the contraction *it's.*

Unit 5 Answer Key

Student Name: _______________________________

Question	Correct Answer	Content Focus	Complexity
1	D	Greek Roots	DOK 2
2	see below	Character, Setting, Plot: Compare and Contrast	DOK 2
3A	B	Idioms	DOK 2
3B	D	Idioms / Text Evidence	DOK 2
4A	C	Greek Roots	DOK 2
4B	A	Greek Roots / Text Evidence	DOK 2
5	B	Character, Setting, Plot: Compare and Contrast	DOK 2
6A	C	Author's Point of View	DOK 3
6B	A	Author's Point of View / Text Evidence	DOK 2
7	A	Text Features: Headings	DOK 1
8A	C	Root Words	DOK 2
8B	D, E	Root Words / Text Evidence	DOK 2
9	see below	Text Structure: Cause and Effect	DOK 2
10	see below	Text Features: Chart	DOK 2
11A	B	Author's Point of View	DOK 3
11B	B	Author's Point of View / Text Evidence	DOK 2
12A	C	Root Words	DOK 2
12B	D	Root Words / Text Evidence	DOK 2
13	A	Text Structure: Cause and Effect	DOK 2
14	see below	Idioms	DOK 2
15	D	Text Features: Diagram	DOK 2
16	B	Clauses	DOK 1
17	A	Using *More* and *Most*	DOK 1

Unit 5 Answer Key   Student Name: _______________________

Question	Correct Answer	Content Focus	Complexity
18	D	Appositives	DOK 1
19	C	Comparing with *Good* and *Bad*	DOK 1
20	D	Capitalization and Punctuation	DOK 1

Comprehension 2, 5, 6A, 6B, 7, 9, 10, 11A, 11B, 13, 15	/18	%
Vocabulary 1, 3A, 3B, 4A, 4B, 8A, 8B, 12A, 12B, 14	/12	%
English Language Conventions 16, 17, 18, 19, 20	/5	%
Total Unit 5 Assessment Score	/35	%

2 Students should complete the chart as follows:

- Kostas: humble, on the quiet side
- Christos: boastful, talkative
- Both: Greek, excited about the Olympics

9 Students should complete the cause-and-effect chain as follows:

- First box: Stephen Bishop, Mat Bransford, and Nick Bransford explored Mammoth Cave.
- Second box: Many of the cave's passageways, rooms, and rock formations were discovered and named.
- Third box: The explorers became familiar with the cave's geology and animal life.
- Fourth box: The three young men could give knowledgeable tours of the cave.

10 **2-point response:** The Wild Cave tour is the most difficult. It lasts 6 hours, covers 5 miles, and involves crawling through caves. The Mammoth Passage tour is easiest. It lasts only 1¼ hours and goes ¾ mile through the largest rooms.

14 Students should underline the following (or similar) context clues:

- "she supervises"
- "You can make this happen"

Unit 5 Answer Key   Student Name: _______________________

Informational Performance Task

Question	Answer	Complexity	Score
1	see below	DOK 2	/1
2	see below	DOK 3	/2
3	see below	DOK 3	/2
Informational Article	see below	DOK 4	/4 [P/O] /4 [E/E] /2 [C]
Total Score			**/15**

1   Students should match the following main ideas and details:

   • **Source #1 Main Idea:** Once introduced to an environment, non-native wildlife can rapidly reproduce.
   Source #3 Detail: "Their numbers can explode."
   • **Source #1 Main Idea:** Removing non-native wildlife can be a challenging task.
   Source #3 Detail: "Once these invaders take hold, they are difficult to eliminate."
   • **Source #1 Main Idea:** Citizens must work together to prevent the spread of non-native plants.
   Source #3 Detail: "People can play a key role in limiting this serious problem."

2   **2-point response:** In Source #1, farmers hoped to use the Asian carp to eat unwanted plants that crowded their ponds. Unfortunately, the carp made it out of the ponds and into larger waterways. Their appearance disrupted the balance of these rivers and lakes.

   In Source #2, Eugene Schieffelin wanted to introduce all of the birds from William Shakespeare's writings into the United States. While many of the birds did not survive, the starling did. It quickly overpowered native birds, destroyed crops, and dirtied public areas.

3   **2-point response:** It is important to stop the spread of invasive plants and animals because once it starts, it is very hard to control or stop. Source #1 tells about the difficulties scientists have encountered blocking carp from Lake Michigan. Source #2 tells how the many efforts to control the starlings have failed. Source #3 tells how the numbers of invasive species can grow quickly and greatly.

10-point anchor paper: Living things have certain habitats. When a new plant or animal is brought into the habitat, the food web is changed. This means that some animals or plants will become food for the new living thing. The population of some animals or plants will decrease.

Sometimes people bring animals to the U.S. to control or get rid of living things that are not wanted in an area. According to Source #1, this is the case of the Asian carp. They were brought to eat algae from the lakes and ponds where catfish are raised. The farmers who brought them had not thought about what would happen if the fish were introduced into other bodies of water. When that did happen, the population of carp increased and the population of small fish decreased. The food web was changed. Some animal and plant populations decreased.

People who want exotic animals for pets must think about what could happen if the animals escaped from their habitat. These animals could destroy the balance of life in many different habitats. This could cause the loss of animals and plants that are used as food for other living things. People need to understand the effects these animals could have on all living things in the environment.

Sometimes new plants or animals are introduced into a habitat by accident. This may happen when people move seeds from one place to another. It can also happen by moving firewood. Sometimes new plants and animals are introduced into a habit with good purposes. This is what happened with the starling. However, adding this bird did more than bring a Shakespeare bird to North America. It caused problems for other birds and the populations in the area.

There are currently about 4,300 invasive species living in North America. Once they are here, it is difficult to get rid of these living things. However, we can prevent adding to the list of invaders by being careful with what we bring into our environment.

Unit 5 Rationales

1

A is incorrect because neither the meaning of the root nor the immediate context of the sentence supports this definition of *chronic*.

B is incorrect because, even though the root refers to time, other sentence clues ("most of his life") suggest that a chronic injury happens for a long time.

C is incorrect because this definition has no connection to the meaning of the root.

D is correct because both the meaning of the root and the context of the paragraph support it.

2

These answers are correct due to evidence of characterization in the text, including narration and dialogue. Kostas is humble because he doesn't brag about his athletic ability. He's on the quiet side because he responds very little to Christos's attempts at conversation. Both are Greek: the narrator mentions that Kostas lives in Athens and calls Greece "his country"; Christos mentions his father's lifelong friendship with the Greek athlete Spyridon Louis. Both are excited about the Olympics because Kostas directly mentions his excitement in a thought, while Christos eagerly chats about the athletes. Christos is boastful and talkative because he keeps telling Christos about his knowledge of the athletes and doesn't seem to stop.

3A

A is incorrect because the long jumper is likely in good shape if he plans to compete in the Olympics.

B is correct because being "out of the woods" means being out of difficulty in this context.

C is incorrect because "out of the woods" is an idiomatic expression; this answer interprets the phrase literally.

D is incorrect because this is not the meaning of the idiom "out of the woods"; Christos never suggests that the long jumper is being untruthful.

3B

A is incorrect because the long jumper's country of origin has no relation to the meaning of "out of the woods."

B is incorrect because the phrase "most of his life" does not suggest that "out of the woods" means "out of difficulty."

C is incorrect because the phrase "He claims" does not suggest that "out of the woods" means "out of difficulty."

D is correct because the phrase "permanently healed" suggests that the long jumper is "out of the woods," or "out of difficulty" and able to compete in the Olympics.

4A

A is incorrect because the cacophony described happens just after Kostas cheers for Spyridon Louis.

B is incorrect because it does not make sense in context; the author describes Spyridon Louis's winning performance, not the poor performance of other competitors.

C is correct because the author describes "thunderous applause and cheering" in the previous paragraph.

D is incorrect because this answer does not relate to the root *phon*, which means "sound."

4B

A is correct because the phrase "exploded in thunderous cheering and applause" describes the *cacophony* referred to in the following paragraph.

B is incorrect because *cacophony* refers to sound; the throwing of hats and other items would create a mess, not a cacophony.

C is incorrect because Christos's voice is never described as loud or noisy.

D is incorrect because the description of a tightly packed crowd does not support the answer in part A that *cacophony* refers to the sounds of shouting and clapping.

5

A is incorrect because the spectators are extremely engaged in watching the marathon.

B is correct because the story mostly takes place in the moments leading up to the marathon finish; the story ends before Kostas and Christos attend the swimming event that they discuss.

C is incorrect because Kostas feels excited and lucky before the marathon finish.

D is incorrect because the author provides no information about how crowded the swimming event will be.

6A

A is incorrect because the author does not suggest that going on the tour is a big risk—even though he or she would likely agree that a tour of the cave is worthwhile.

B is incorrect because the author describes several features other than the Star Chamber and expresses no preference.

C is correct because the author portrays Mammoth Cave's overall story as the history of its explorers and tour guides.

D is incorrect because the author gives no explicit opinion about the U.S. National Park Service; given the author's positive attitude toward the cave and its current tours, his or her opinion is probably the opposite.

6B

A is correct because the sentence shows that the caves would not have been explored if not for the bravery of the early guides.

B is incorrect because the sentence does not support the idea that the early guides were important to the cave's exploration.

C is incorrect because the sentence does not support the idea that the early guides were important to the cave's exploration.

D is incorrect because the sentence does not support the idea that the early guides were important to the cave's exploration.

7

A is correct because each heading tells part of the story of Mammoth Cave: its explorers, the tours they gave, and the involvement of the U.S. Park Service.

B is incorrect because the headings make no reference to either man.

C is incorrect because two of the three headings introduce events that occurred before the National Park Service took over.

D is incorrect because the headings make no reference to the cave's natural features.

8A

A is incorrect because the Latin root *terra* does not relate to sight or darkness, and the paragraph states that many of the subterranean creatures do not have eyes.

B is incorrect because the Latin root *terra* does not relate to the definition.

C is correct because the Latin root *terra*, along with the prefix *sub-*, suggests that the word *subterranean* means "under earth," or "underground.

D is incorrect because the Latin root *terra* does not relate to the definition.

8B

A is incorrect because the sentence does not clearly support the answer to part A that *subterranean* means "underground."

B is incorrect because the sentence does not clearly support the answer to part A that *subterranean* means "underground."

C is incorrect because the sentence does not clearly support the answer to part A that *subterranean* means "underground."

D is correct because the sentence describes an "underground river," which supports the answer to part A that *subterranean* means "underground."

E is correct because the sentence describes "pitch black" caverns, which supports the answer to part A that *subterranean* means "underground."

F is incorrect because the sentence does not support the answer to part A that *subterranean* means "underground."

9

These answers are correct because they show three sequential, direct causal links.

10

See answer key for sample response.

11A

A is incorrect because the author suggests that it is important to give kids certain responsibilities.

B is correct because the author's central point in paragraph 2 is about kids becoming "eager learners . . . who seek information" at libraries and nurseries.

C is incorrect because the author mentions the importance of adults supporting children's learning.

D is incorrect because the author does not mention learning outside the context of the community garden.

11B

A is incorrect because the sentence does not specify what the "benefits" are; therefore, it is not the best support for the answer in part A.

B is correct because the sentence explains that kids become "eager learners" when they are able to "take ownership of something," which supports the statement in part A that giving kids responsibilities will "make them excited to learn more."

C is incorrect because the sentence is about residents' engagement in the community, not about how giving kids responsibilities will "make them excited to learn more."

D is incorrect because the sentence is about how kids' involvement means their families' involvement too, not about how giving kids responsibilities will "make them excited to learn more."

12A

A is incorrect because the author makes no reference to vegetarianism or veganism, and the context of the paragraph does not support this meaning.

B is incorrect because the author makes no reference to "nature preserves," and the context of the paragraph does not support this meaning.

C is correct because produce is generally grown in a field, and the context of the paragraph and text as a whole supports this meaning.

D is incorrect because the meaning of *agr* ("field") has nothing to do with learning about a topic.

12B

A is incorrect because the sentence is about kids showing ownership, not about "the practice of using land to grow food."

B is incorrect because the sentence is about families caring about local issues, not about "the practice of using land to grow food."

C is incorrect because the sentence is about community engagement, not about "the practice of using land to grow food."

D is correct because the sentence relates to the definition of agriculture—the practice of using land to grow food.

13

A is correct because the paragraph is organized as a cause-effect chain: since kids are associated with adults, they will involve more community members in gardening, which will result in greater community engagement.

B is incorrect because the author does not mention that a community garden with kids will attract more people to the town.

C is incorrect because the author does not mention that a community garden with kids will produce more varieties of healthy food.

D is incorrect because the author explains that kids will learn about waste removal, not that more waste will necessarily be created.

14

The context clue "She supervises" shows that the girl knows all about how to plant seeds—enough to supervise others doing it.

The context clue "You can make this happen" shows that the author is turning over responsibility for acting on his/her idea to the Jonesville City Council.

15

A is incorrect because the diagram does not make any clear connection between the community gardens and public health.

B is incorrect because the diagram does not show different types of seeds.

C is incorrect because the diagram shows children; the author states that Jonesville requires community members to be at least eighteen to apply for a plot.

D is correct because the diagram shows a girl teaching her brother how to use the garden plot, as described in paragraph 4.

16

A is incorrect because people give the answer *to* a question, not *of* a question.

B is correct because a comma is standard to indicate a pause and to separate a phrase beginning with *if* from the rest of the sentence.

C is incorrect because acronyms like *DNA* must be capitalized.

D is incorrect because the sentence contains an error in comma usage; the comma should come at the end of the dependent clause.

17

A is correct because the word *handiest* is a superlative adjective; *most* and *-est* should never be used with the same adjective.

B is incorrect because it is not grammatical to use *most* with the comparative adjective *handier*.

C is incorrect because the sentence is grammatically awkward; the sentence calls for a superlative adjective.

D is incorrect because *more* and *-est* should never be used with the same adjective.

18

A is incorrect because it does not contain an appositive.

B is incorrect because it does not contain an appositive.

C is incorrect because it does not contain a verb and incorporates an appositive incorrectly.

D is correct because it contains an appositive and combines the sentences in a grammatically correct way.

19

A is incorrect because adding a semicolon introduces a fragment, and the sentence still contains an error (*gooder*).

B is incorrect because the dash appropriately sets apart a section of the sentence for emphasis, and the sentence still contains an error (*gooder*).

C is correct because *good* takes the irregular comparative *better*.

D is incorrect because *good* takes the irregular comparative *better*.

20

A is incorrect because a comma is grammatically correct after *2008*, and the sentence contains two capitalization errors.

B is incorrect because it introduces an error (*its* is being used as a possessive, not as a contraction) and neglects to correct the capitalization error.

C is incorrect because it introduces an error (2008 is only one year, so the singular possessive *year's* should stay as is) and neglects to correct the capitalization error.

D is correct because the titles of long texts such as magazines take an initial capital letter.

   Unit Assessments

Unit 6 Answer Key

Student Name: ________________________________

Question	Correct Answer	Content Focus	Complexity
1A	A	Context Clues: Paragraph Clues	DOK 2
1B	B	Context Clues: Paragraph Clues / Text Evidence	DOK 2
2A	B	Point of View	DOK 2
2B	A	Point of View / Text Evidence	DOK 2
3	D	Personification	DOK 2
4	see below	Literary Elements: Flashback	DOK 2
5	C	Theme	DOK 3
6	see below	Text Structure: Cause and Effect	DOK 3
7A	D	Context Clues: Paragraph Clues	DOK 2
7B	B	Context Clues: Paragraph Clues / Text Evidence	DOK 2
8	see below	Homophones	DOK 1
9A	A	Text Structure: Cause and Effect	DOK 2
9B	B	Text Structure: Cause and Effect / Text Evidence	DOK 2
10A	D	Text Structure: Cause and Effect	DOK 2
10B	B	Text Structure: Cause and Effect / Text Evidence	DOK 2
11A	D	Context Clues: Paragraph Clues	DOK 2
11B	C	Context Clues: Paragraph Clues / Text Evidence	DOK 2
12	see below	Personification	DOK 2
13	A, E	Point of View	DOK 2
14	C	Lyric Poetry	DOK 2
15A	D	Theme	DOK 3
15B	A	Theme / Text Evidence	DOK 3
16	B	Using *more, most*	DOK 1
17	D	Sentence Combining	DOK 1

Unit 6 Answer Key   Student Name: _______________________________

Question	Correct Answer	Content Focus	Complexity
18	C	Conjunctive Adverbs	DOK 1
19	C	Pronouns in Prepositional Phrases	DOK 1
20	B	Correct Double Negatives	DOK 1

Comprehension 2A, 2B, 4, 5, 6, 9A, 9B, 10A, 10B, 13, 14, 15A, 15B	/18	%
Vocabulary 1A, 1B, 3, 7A, 7B, 8, 11A, 11B, 12	/12	%
English Language Conventions 16, 17, 18, 19, 20	/5	%
Total Unit 6 Assessment Score	/35	%

4 Students should check the following boxes for each information statement in the chart:
- Amelia Earhart crosses the Atlantic Ocean in an airplane. — Revealed During Flashback
- Charlie shares a milkshake. — Revealed During Regular Action
- The ranch owner leads tours of the Double D. — Revealed During Regular Action

6 **2-point response:** Blackwell's father made sure that Elizabeth and her siblings had tutors in "challenging subjects like mathematics and Latin." When the family moved from England to America, Blackwell's studies continued in an "excellent school." Her father's belief that women should have a "wide education" helped prepare her to become a doctor.

8 Students should circle the word "allowed."

12 Students should mark the following boxes in the chart:
- "O'er pleasant fields and dusty lanes, / Where I would race and romp and shout"—no personification
- "But heart and mind were far away, / Engaged in some glad bit of play."—heart, mind
- "It seemed the clock upon the wall / From hour to hour could only crawl,"—clock

Unit 6 Answer Key   Student Name: ___________________________

Opinion Performance Task			
Question	**Answer**	**Complexity**	**Score**
1	see below	DOK 2	/1
2	see below	DOK 3	/2
3	see below	DOK 3	/2
Opinion Article	see below	DOK 4	/4 [P/O] /4 [E/E] /2 [C]
Total Score			**/15**

1   Students should select the following:
  • Source #1: "In time, few seedlings were found near wells."
  • Source #2: "Around the world, the numbers of this insect have dropped."

2   **2-point response:** People can help reduce the negative impact we have on plants and animals by making changes. In Source #1: "An Invisible Pollution," the author points out that turning down the volume on machines and shutting of things we aren't using can help. In Source #2: "Our Dark Night Sky," the author notes that many people are turning off lights they are not using to avoid confusing birds and other flying animals, especially when they are migrating.

3   **2-point response:** In Source #1: "An Invisible Pollution" and Source #2: "Our Dark Night Sky," the authors discuss how man-made changes have created a negative impact on the environment. However, in Source #3: "Understanding Dams," the author explains the benefits of dams to people. He or she discusses ways that we can keep using this resource while reducing its negative effect on the environment.

10-point anchor paper: Our county is debating whether or not to build a new highway outside of town. People are concerned about how this will affect the wildlife in the area, and for good reason. The new highway could change the behaviors of many animals living nearby. However, we have learned so much about how light and noise affect wildlife. I believe we can find solutions to the problems this project presents. The best time to build this highway is now, when the community is thinking about the impact on the environment. That way, we can find ways to make the highway have less of an impact on local wildlife.

We have learned a lot about how light from highways affects the environment. Perhaps we can find a solution for this, such as motion-activated streetlights or an unlighted overpass for animals. That way, animals like the puma will not see the highway as a boundary that limits where it can travel for food. Motion-activated lights would also save energy and be less likely to confuse migrating birds.

The noise of construction and of vehicles on the new highway is also an issue. However, perhaps we can find ways to limit the effect of this noise on the environment. For example, plants and dirt banks could soak up most of the noise before it travels far from the road. Finally, the construction of a new dam will have a large impact on the environment. Because much of the water from the wetland will be contained in the dammed area, volunteers will be needed to move some plants and animals to the new wetland area. This may preserve species that otherwise might not survive. Finally, if we use our dam as a clean energy source, we can reduce noise and light created by other power sources.

Some may say that these steps do not solve the whole problem. However, I believe our goal should be to try to live in harmony with the environment. Given the lifestyle people are used to, this will have to happen in a series of small steps. There is no way to erase the mark we have made on the environment, so we need to take great care. We need to think carefully about how our actions will impact it and taking steps to preserve it.

Unit 6 Rationales

1A

A is correct because "lowly" is the meaning of the word *humble* in this context.

B is incorrect because "unlucky" is not the meaning of the word *humble*.

C is incorrect because "difficult" is not the meaning of the word *humble*.

D is incorrect because "unique" is not the meaning of the word *humble*, and this definition does not make sense in context.

1B

A is incorrect because "unbelievable that this happened" explains how Charlie feels about the situation, not why he describes his station in life as humble.

B is correct because Charlie clarifies that he is "just a junior ranch hand" after saying that he has a humble station in life.

C is incorrect because the phrase "witnesses to prove" is unrelated to Charlie's "humble station in life."

D is incorrect because "split a shake" tells how Earhart shared a milkshake with Charlie; it does not explain why he describes his station in life as humble.

2A

A is incorrect because the story does not compare Earhart's popularity in Meeteetse with her popularity in other areas.

B is correct because phrases from the narrator ("luckiest eleven-year-old boy on this magnificent planet," "she and her plane are laughing," "ran to tell all the boys," "hightailed it to . . . buy a new shirt," and "my jaw dropped so low") do indeed give the story an energetic and star-struck feel.

C is incorrect because the plot events are not all sequential; the story contains a flashback.

D is incorrect because the first-person narration denies the reader access to the thoughts of other characters besides Charlie.

2B

A is correct because this sentence shows the narrator's youthful energy and enthusiasm toward Earhart.

B is incorrect because this sentence does not necessarily show the narrator's youthful enthusiasm toward Earhart.

C is incorrect because this sentence merely has the narrator recalling something he heard.

D is incorrect because this sentence does not necessarily show the narrator's youthful enthusiasm toward Earhart.

3

A is incorrect because Earhart does not actually say this quote; Charlie is quoting from his own imagination.

B is incorrect because the sentences do not make a comparison.

C is incorrect because the sentences do not indicate the likelihood that something will happen later in the text; they are about something that has already happened.

D is correct because Charlie uses his imagination to ascribe human characteristics (*laughing* and *thinking*) to a nonhuman object (the plane).

4

Row 1: This information is revealed during the italicized flashback in paragraph 5.

Row 2: This information is revealed in multiple paragraphs (1 and 14) during the regular action.

Row 3: This information is revealed during the regular action in paragraph 10.

5

A is incorrect because the text does not suggest that this tendency of cowpokes is necessarily a good tendency to have.

B is incorrect because the main point of the text is not that young people tend to exaggerate; rather, the narration of the story indicates young characters' excitement.

C is correct because the text shows how Charlie's world gets rocked when a famous person happens to stay at his place of employment.

D is incorrect because none of the characters allow their pride to prevent them from marveling at Earhart.

6

See answer key for sample response.

7A

A is incorrect because "follow close behind" is the definition of *pursue* when used in a different context; this definition does not make sense in the sentence.

B is incorrect because "create a change" does not make sense in the context of the sentence.

C is incorrect because "learn all about" does not make sense in the context of the text.

D is correct because "try to achieve" is the definition of *pursue* as it is used in the sentence.

7B

A is incorrect because the sentence is referring to Blackwell's career as a teacher, not the new goal she decided to pursue.

B is correct because the sentence explains exactly how Blackwell started to pursue a career in medicine.

C is incorrect because the sentence is more focused on the male students' treatment of her at medical school than her pursuit of a new career.

D is incorrect because the sentence is focused on Blackwell's success in obtaining a medical degree, not her initial pursuit of a career in medicine.

8

The word *allowed* is a homophone of the word *aloud,* which means "in a voice that can be heard" or "loudly."

9A

A is correct because Blackwell's persistence in the face of obstacles is one of the focuses of the text.

B is incorrect because the author states that Blackwell politely ignored classmates who would throw paper airplanes at her.

C is incorrect because the author does not compare her study habits to those of other classmates.

D is incorrect because the author never states that Blackwell tried to prove she was the smartest student in class.

9B

A is incorrect because the sentence does not discuss any specific obstacles that Blackwell faced.

B is correct because the sentence specifically states how Blackwell kept trying when professors opposed her.

C is incorrect because the sentence does not discuss any specific obstacles that Blackwell faced.

D is incorrect because the sentence does not discuss any specific obstacles that Blackwell faced.

10A

A is incorrect because other women would have faced similar struggles.

B is incorrect because Blackwell's fame is less important than her ability to effect change.

C is incorrect because Blackwell did not have to prove that women were fine teachers; according to the text, a teacher "was one of the few acceptable careers for a woman."

D is correct because the author's purpose in describing the public's opinion is to show that "the views of a woman's abilities were shifting" thanks to Blackwell.

10B

A is incorrect because the sentence is not specific enough in supporting the author's point that Blackwell helped the public accept the idea of women doctors.

B is correct because the sentence includes a specific detail showing how Blackwell helped people accept the idea of women doctors—that "several more medical schools accepted women students."

C is incorrect because the sentence does not support the author's point that Blackwell helped the public accept the idea of women doctors.

D is incorrect because the sentence does not support the author's point that Blackwell helped the public accept the idea of women doctors.

11A

A is incorrect because "nervousness" does not make sense in context; nervousness would not come to the speaker's cheeks.

B is incorrect because "thought" does not make sense in context; a thought would not come to the speaker's cheeks.

C is incorrect because "fever" does not make sense in context; the speaker would not get a fever from getting caught daydreaming.

D is correct because *crimson* is a color that means "purplish-red"; the speaker is embarrassed from getting caught daydreaming.

11B

A is incorrect because the word *mind* does not point to the definition of *crimson*.

B is incorrect because the word *Wool* does not point to the definition of *crimson*.

C is correct because the word *blushing* helps to explain that *crimson* means "purplish-red."

D is incorrect because the word *dream* does not point to the definition of *crimson*.

12

"O'er pleasant fields and dusty lanes / Where I would race and romp and shout" does not contain personification; the speaker does not give the fields and lanes human qualities.

In the line "But heart and mind were far away / Engaged in some glad bit of play," "heart" and "mind" are personified because the speaker describes them as "playing," which is something that humans do.

In the line "It seemed the clock upon the wall / From hour to hour could only crawl," "clock" is personified because the speaker describes it as "crawling."

13

A is correct because the speaker cannot know the feelings of other students; he does not include quotations or evidence to show their feelings.

B is incorrect because the speaker *does* identify the existence of the clock on the wall; he has a view of it from where he sits.

C is incorrect because the speaker *does* include the teacher's reaction by providing a quotation from her.

D is incorrect because the speaker *does* include details from his dream.

E is correct because the speaker cannot know the teacher's general opinion of him; the quotation that the speaker includes does not reveal anything about what she thinks of him as a person.

F is incorrect because the speaker *does* explain how much time is left in the scene he recalls: "The last two weeks dragged slowly by."

   Unit Assessments

14

A is incorrect because the rhyme scheme has nothing to do with the length of the school year.

B is incorrect because the rhyme scheme itself does not have the overall effect of aiding visualization; rather, some of the rhyming words simply refer to physical objects in the room.

C is correct because end rhyme is common in songs, and the rhyming in the poem makes it more cheerful to match the speaker's youthful excitement about summer.

D is incorrect because neither the rhyming words (nor the scheme of end rhyme itself) points readers to the most important words thematically.

15A

A is incorrect because the speaker feels frustrated and enclosed in his surroundings; he wishes to be elsewhere.

B is incorrect because the speaker is daydreaming rather than eagerly learning his lessons.

C is incorrect because the speaker does not describe or refer to anything nearly as unpleasant as pain.

D is correct because the poem is about daydreaming in anticipation of summer.

15B

A is correct because the lines describe the speaker excitedly daydreaming about the fun he would have once school ended for the year.

B is incorrect because the lines are about the speaker's frustration that school is still in session, not his daydreaming.

C is incorrect because the lines are about the moment the speaker gets caught daydreaming, rather than his feelings of anticipation for the summer.

D is incorrect because the lines are about the teacher catching the speaker daydreaming, rather than his feelings of anticipation for the summer.

16

A is incorrect because *Josefa* is a singular noun, so the possessive *Josefa's* is correct.

B is correct because the correct adverb that compares is *more*; in order for the word *most* to be correct, the sentence would have to read "... people admired Josefa's bowls the most."

C is incorrect because the word *else's* needs to remain possessive.

D is incorrect because the sentence contains the wrong adverb and the word *else's* needs to remain possessive.

17

A is incorrect because the phrase "was standing there too" is redundant.

B is incorrect because Josefa and Carmen are standing together near the bench, and this combination awkwardly separates them within the sentence.

C is incorrect because it unnecessarily creates a very long sentence, and the phrase "was standing there too" is redundant.

D is correct because it deletes the redundant phrase "was standing there too" and elegantly condenses the two sentences.

18

A is incorrect because the conjunctive adverb *similarly* does not make sense in the context of the paragraph; Josefa is not making a comparison.

B is incorrect because the conjunctive adverb *otherwise* incorrectly describes the relationship between sentences 10 and 11.

C is correct because the conjunctive adverb *however* correctly describes the contrasting relationship between sentences 10 and 11.

D is incorrect because the conjunctive adjective *still* incorrectly describes the relationship between sentences 10 and 11.

19

A is incorrect because the antecedent of the pronoun in the prepositional phrase is *Josefa*, so the pronoun should be the singular feminine pronoun *her* instead of *them*.

B is incorrect because the story is written in the past tense, not the present tense, and because *she* is the incorrect pronoun.

C is correct because the pronoun following the preposition *for* had to be changed in case.

D is incorrect because *they* is a subject pronoun; the sentence requires an object pronoun that agrees with the singular feminine antecedent *Josefa*.

20

A is incorrect because *didn't* is already spelled correctly, and because it doesn't correct the double negative in the sentence.

B is correct because it corrects the double negative.

C is incorrect because Isidora is not asking a question, and because it doesn't correct the double negative.

D is incorrect because *everything* is the incorrect indefinite pronoun to use in the sentence.